HORSE-RACING
AND RACING SOCIETY

To my brother, Crispin,
without whom racing would be dull

HORSE-RACING AND RACING SOCIETY

Who belongs and How it Works

Jocelyn de Moubray

SIDGWICK & JACKSON
LONDON

First published in Great Britain in 1985 by
Sidgwick & Jackson Limited

Copyright © 1985 by Jocelyn de Moubray

ISBN 0-283-99097-X

Printed in Great Britain by
The Garden City Press, Letchworth, Hertfordshire
for Sidgwick & Jackson Limited
1 Tavistock Chambers, Bloomsbury Way
London WC1A 2SG

Contents

Acknowledgements

I would like to thank the following for their help: The Hon. Robert Acton, The Hon. Sir John Astor, Ian Balding, Mrs Ian Balding, Mrs Desmond Baring, Charles Benson, Maurice Camacho, David Cecil, N.S.C. Collin, Lt-Col J.A. Cooke, Mrs J.A. Cooke, Humphrey Cottrill, Tony Couch, Messrs Coutts & Co, James Delahooke, William Elsey, Philip Freedman, Brigadier Henry Green, William Haggas, The Earl of Halifax, Lady Halifax, Ruth, Countess of Halifax, Colonel Peter Hamer, Guy Harwood, Michael Harris, William Hastings Bass, Christopher Hill, John Hislop, Mrs John Hislop, John Hamner, Annie Horton, Lord Howard de Walden, Ryan Jarvis, Libby Joy, Dr Paul Khan, Richard Kilburn, Sir Timothy Kitson, Lady Kitson, Dieter Klein, Pauline Lambton, Sir David Llewellyn, Sir Robin McAlpine, Hugh Macdonald Buchanan, Lt-Col Tom Nickals, Major Peter Nelson, Mrs Peter Nelson, Charles Nugent, Anthony Oppenheimer, The Maharajah of Rajpipla, Nicholas Robinson, Pat Rohan, Guy Sangster, Peter Scott, David Simmonds and Heathorns Ltd, Major David Swannell, Jeremy Tree, Frank Vogel, Marcus Wickham Boynton, Margo Winnick; and for their support: Rory Carnegie, Quentin Crewe, Lucy Marshall, Nicholas Milner, Adam Seccombe, Ian Watson, The Lady Susan Watson, Amicia de Moubray, and Guy and Daphne de Moubray.

Introduction

One hundred years ago the purpose of horse-racing was solely the indulgence of those aristocrats and men of established power and money who chose to own racehorses. These patrons not only had enough leisure to spend many days on the racecourse, but were themselves expert in the breeding and training of the racehorse. They raced horses that they had bred themselves and employed their own trainers and jockeys, though few of these professionals gained more esteem than that given to a trustworthy butler. If the public were allowed to observe the sport, they were not encouraged to do so. Admiral Rous carefully arranged that each race at Newmarket finished at a different place so that only those who were in contact with the administration were able to follow the proceedings.

Today it is rare for knowledge and expertise in racing to coincide with the wealth that is a prerequisite for owning the best racehorse. The owner, ceasing to be a patron, has become a consumer. He buys his horse from a professional breeder with the help of a bloodstock agent, before sending it to a trainer who has virtual control over the animal's career. The considerable prestige enjoyed by the leading trainers is independent of their owners, and numerous articles are written about a particular stable's hopes for the new season with little reference to those who pay the bills. The top jockeys enjoy a similar independence. For a time they were tied to a particular stable rather than to a particular owner, but following Lester Piggott's decision to split with Noel Murless in 1966 and to rely upon informal arrangements for his mounts, it has become accepted that jockeys need not be tied to anyone, even if many choose to be for reasons of security.

The change in the relationships between owners, trainers, and jockeys has never been more clearly illustrated than in the winner's enclosure after the 1984 St Leger. Lester Piggott rode the winner Commanche Run, thus achieving a record number of classic victories, only after he had persuaded the colt's owner and trainer to break a contract they had made with Darrell McHargue to ride the stable's horses. John Oaksey conducted a television interview in the winner's enclosure immediately after the race – something that would have been considered scandalous in itself until recently – which was centred on Lester Piggott. The horse's trainer, Luca Cumani, was allowed to make a few comments, but the owner Ivan Allen was not even mentioned.

To own racehorses was at one time a sign of established power and prestige. Now, it is becoming either a means of achieving such a position, or a means of making money. As the type of person who owns racehorses has changed, as well as the reasons that they do so, the roles and rewards of the rest of the racing world – the trainers, jockeys, stable lads, breeders, and administrators – have adjusted correspondingly. The racehorse itself, moreover, has undergone a fundamental transformation. There was a time when it was possible to tell from looking at a horse's breeding whether it was likely to do its racing at Catterick Bridge or at Ascot. A handful of stallions were markedly superior at producing the most esteemed racehorse, which was able to compete with the best over a mile and a half as a three-year-old, before reaching its peak as a four-year-old, when it was expected to compete for the cup races, run over distances in excess of two miles. Today there are two or three hundred stallions scattered throughout the world who are perfectly capable of producing a Derby winner, all of whom have impeccable pedigrees; none of them, with the exception of Northern Dancer, are markedly superior to their contemporaries. There was a time when most equine generations were dominated by one or two horses of an unmistakably superior mould. Yet there has not been a horse since Brigadier Gerard in the early 1970s that has dominated his contemporaries for three seasons.

The pattern of contemporary racing is for particularly fast-developing horses to dominate as two-year-olds. They are then overtaken by horses that reach their peak in the spring of their three-year-old career, the time of the Guineas and the Epsom classic races, only for these spring horses to be overtaken by the time of the important autumn races. The superior racehorse has become immensely fragile: El Gran Señor was undoubtedly a very fast racehorse but he displayed this on only one occasion, his memorable victory in the 1984 Two Thousand Guineas, and he was unable to stand the strain of training after the summer of his three-year-old career.

Once a symbol of power and grace, the racehorse has become little more than a fragile symbol of money. To look upon horse-racing as an establishment event, to take the traditional aspects of its rituals as anything more than nostalgia, is to ignore what has happened over the last ten years. This nostalgia is still strong, and the daily rituals of the paddock and the winner's enclosure – which are as much a parade of owners, *aficionados*, and officials as of horses – preserve the distinction between observers and the observed. Racing is still administered by the Jockey Club, a self-electing and socially homogeneous body. However, the true split in the racing world is between those who are involved in the business of buying and selling horses, and those who are in the business of selling entertainment to those who follow racing in the betting shop and on television.

If this is an unappealing situation, it is interesting to speculate whether the recent Arab investment in racehorses may not mark the end of the commercial era of racing. Horse-racing in Britain, and throughout the world, is at a moment of crisis. The crisis is not financial, but one of structure and purpose. The breeding and racing of horses are commercial to an extent that would have appeared incredible only ten years ago: 1984 saw the Derby being won by a colt making his third and final appearance on the racecourse; Sheikh Mohammed giving 3,100,000 Irish guineas for a yearling by the deceased Shergar; and a share in the American stallion Seattle Slew being sold for a figure that gave him a nominal value of $150 million. It is widely accepted, however, that commercialism on this scale cannot continue. Not only is the appeal of racing as a spectacle in danger, but many of those upon whom racing relies – the small owners, trainers, and breeders – are being forced to withdraw from the industry by financial constraints. What are the possible outcomes of this crisis and, in the first place, how did it arise?

1

The Golden Age of English Racing

The closing decades of the nineteenth century have often been described as the 'golden age' of English racing. It was the last time racing was dominated by the horses of a few aristocrats, and the last time all the leading racing figures of the day were English, with the exception of the Scottish trainer Matthew Dawson. The élite that indulged in horse-racing was closely allied to the ruling political élite. In 1894 Lord Rosebery, then serving British Prime Minister, was successful in the Derby. Lord Randolph Churchill, Lord Hartington, the Marquis of Londonderry, the Earl of Zetland, James Lowther, the Earl of Cadogan, and Henry Chaplin were other members of the Jockey Club who held ministerial posts during this period.

It is possible to speculate that tensions arising from arguments as to the proper aims of Imperialism within the Liberal leadership were diffused by some gentle talk of horses – setting a precedent for what Dubai's Defence Minister has said now takes place at meetings of Middle Eastern Defence Ministers. More importantly, by this time the Jockey Club had not only asserted its right to administer racing, but had also managed to enforce standardized procedures and codes of conduct. Racing was no longer blatantly corrupt.

This was a period of a few outstanding horses; St Simon, Ormonde, and Persimmon have all been mythologized by turf historians. To some extent such animals were their owners' champions in a succession of tournaments that made up their racing careers. When the Duke of Portland's St Simon had proved himself to be an outstanding two-year-old, the Duke was challenged by the Duke of Westminster to match St Simon against his best two-year-old at Newmarket. The resulting race proved to be one sided: St Simon was fifty yards in front after only two furlongs. The stories of Ormonde and Persimmon are tales of repeated struggles against almost equal adversaries, Minting and St Frusquin respectively.

If racing maintained some chivalric associations, it was also a popular entertainment, and in Fred Archer it produced a popular idol. Archer was a phenomenally successful jockey. He won a third of the races in which he rode. He won his first race at the age of thirteen, and was champion jockey for the first time only three years later, a position he maintained for the rest of his life. Such figures are even more remarkable when it is considered that from an early age he had to fast continually to maintain a weight of eight stone seven pounds, existing on the occasional glass of champagne and quantities of a potion that became known as Archer's mixture. Archer was reputed to earn eight thousand pounds a year, which is a testimony of his skill in dealing with owners. For eleven years Lord Falmouth had first claim on his services, and with the assistance of the trainer Matthew Dawson they dominated racing, winning twelve classic races in ten years.

Lord Falmouth had inherited his title somewhat unexpectedly upon the death of a cousin. He then set about breeding racehorses at Mereworth Castle, the fine Palladian house his wife had given him. He had no interest in betting, or in winning any other than the very best races, and he bred all his classic winners himself. Archer was in demand from every other leading owner, not only as a jockey, but because he was one of the best judges of form, combining acute observation with an intuitive understanding of the horse. He would advise owners where to run a particular horse, hoping to place it where it would win and he would be able to ride it.

The public's image of Archer was of a man who always tried to win. Despite the fact that he was the subject of public speculation from adolescence on, he was never tempted by dalliance. He was famously parsimonious, living in a room above Dawson's stables until his marriage. He married the daughter of Matthew Dawson's brother and moved into a substantial house he had had built in Newmarket, loyally named Falmouth House. His first child survived only a few hours. Subsequently, tremendously excited when told at Liverpool races that he had a daughter, he rushed back to Newmarket only to find both his wife and daughter dead. He is said never to have recovered, and from then on his friend Captain Bowling slept in the same room as him, as there was always a fear that he might take his own life.

Archer was the first of many jockeys to be a popular hero. What endeared him to the public was his sustained dedication and apparent indifference to both fame and money. One of Archer's few indulgences was his gambling, which was on a prodigious scale, but he was frequently known to ride vigorously to beat his own money. There were attempts to implicate him in some major scandals, particularly after the 1883 Derby in which he was said to have pulled Lord Falmouth's colt Galliard in the hope that this would enable his brother Charles Archer to win the race with a horse that he trained called Highland Chief. Galliard's defeat was said to have hastened Lord Falmouth's retirement from racing, but whatever Archer's intentions it cannot have been a happy race for him, as St Blaise beat both Highland Chief and Galliard.

Archer's final depression came in the autumn of 1886, partly as a result of the effort of riding a fancied horse in the Cambridgeshire at eight stone seven pounds. He was beaten a head and contracted a severe fever. Retiring to bed the following week, he shot himself while under the fever's influence. The pistol he used to do the deed is among the exhibits of the National Horseracing Museum, and apparently arouses more interest than any other.

The two other leading owner-breeders of this period were the Duke of Westminster and the Duke of Portland. The sixth Duke of Portland was extraordinarily lucky to become the sixth Duke, as he inherited the title from a distant cousin, his father having been a second son and his grandfather a third son. At the time, 1879, he was known as William Cavendish Bentick and was serving as a subaltern in the Coldstream Guards. When Cavendish Bentick heard of the death of the fifth Duke he called on his colonel to inform him that he was going on leave. The colonel was out, so he left a message with his batman. On his return the colonel was told that Cavendish Bentick had called to say that he was going on leave, but that he could not have been sober as he called himself the Duke of Portland.

Despite the fact that he lived until 1941, the Duke of Portland was always known as the owner of St Simon. Apparently this did not bother him at all, and as an old man there was nothing he enjoyed doing more than talking about St Simon, declaring that he could not think of anything he would rather be remembered for. He was fortunate to have had the opportunity of buying St Simon. St Simon's breeder, Prince Gustavus Batthyany, an Hungarian by birth though he was naturalized in 1838, was killed by Galliard, the same horse that caused Lord Falmouth to give up racing. Galliard was by Galopin, whom Prince Batthyany had bought as a yearling and of whom he was exceptionally fond, hoping that he would become a successful stallion. Before the Two Thousand Guineas of 1883, in which Galliard was due to run, Prince Batthyany was in a state of excitement, so much so that he collapsed when walking out of the Jockey Club rooms, where he had had lunch, and died.

All the Prince's horses were sold at the July Sales of that year. Among them was a horse called Fulmen, whom the twenty-five-year-old Duke of Portland and his trainer Matthew Dawson decided to buy. Fulmen, however, made 5,000 guineas, which was more than they were prepared to spend. So when the next lot, a brown two-year-old colt by Galopin called St Simon, was led in they decided to bid for him, and bought him for 1,600 guineas.

Sixteen hundred guineas was a lot of money for an untried horse by Galopin, who had not yet fulfilled his late owner's hopes, but there is reason to suppose that Matthew Dawson's brother, who had trained for the Prince, knew of St Simon's potential. Matthew Dawson was unable to find him but was suspicious of the fact that St Simon was extraordinarily fat for a two-year-old that was supposed to be attracting buyers. It seems likely that John Dawson hoped no one would buy him so that he would remain in his care.

St Simon was a horse out of the ordinary. He had the electricity, the nervous energy of a great horse. His groom declared that it was all very well to talk of the patience of Job, but Job had never had to groom St Simon. Archer touched him with his spurs only once, when he was being lazy on the gallops. St Simon reacted by taking off, and Archer was not able to pull him up until they were well into Newmarket. Archer dismounted, saying that St Simon was not a horse but a steam engine. There are probably not many stable lads in Newmarket who habitually compare themselves with biblical figures; nor can there be many jockeys who would use the steam engine as a symbol of power, but then this was the 1880s.

Unable to run in any of the classic races due to the death of his original owner, St Simon won all his nine races without being remotely extended. At this time Dawson trained Harvester and

Busybody, who were St Simon's contemporaries and later to win the Derby and the Oaks respectively. He worked the three together shortly before St Simon's match with the Duke of Westminster's two-year-old, and St Simon finished so far in front that he was sure the other two had lost their form. Yet the following week Busybody won the Middle Park Stakes, then England's most important race for two-year-olds.

At the end of the season the Duke of Portland decided to give St Simon an easy three-year-old career in the hope that he would thus be more potent as a stallion – a consideration of the future that might have been prompted by the potential financial rewards; but, then, St Simon had little to prove on the racecourse. The only race St Simon was really prepared for was the Ascot Gold Cup, which he won by twenty lengths, finishing so full of running that his jockey was unable to pull him up until he had completed another circuit of the track. After easy wins in the Goodwood and Newcastle Cups he was retired to stud, where he was phenomenally successful. When the oldest of his progeny were two-year-olds he was second in the general sires' list, and thereafter he headed the list nine times and sired ten winners of seventeen classic races. Before racing became international the only stallions who came close to such a record were Blandford and Hyperion, who each sired seven classic winners.

After his initial luck the Duke of Portland settled down to racing in the traditional manner, maintaining a large stud at Welbeck, his country house. For a time he was very successful, not least because he had unlimited access to the best stallion, owning eleven classic winners between 1888 and 1900. This profusion of St Simon's blood eventually became a problem, and though he bought an Australian horse, Carbine, as an outcrop, his luck had run out; he did not own another good horse after 1903. The Duke later suffered the ignominy of being asked to remove his horses from Fred Darling's stables. He had so enraged Darling at dinner the night before, with his habit of cracking his knuckles, that the trainer decided he would rather lose the Portland horses than have to repeat the ordeal of having His Grace to dinner.

The first Duke of Westminster, despite the fact that he is the only man to have owned and bred two Triple Crown[1] winners, caused considerably less public comment than his horses. His interest in racing first came to notice when he paid Robert Peck 14,000 guineas for the Derby winner Doncaster in 1876. This was an unprecedented price even for a stallion, but his judgement was proved to be sound when Doncaster's son Bend Or won the Derby for him in 1880. On Peck's retirement he sent his horses to be trained by John Porter in the Kingsclere stables where Ian Balding trains today. John Porter had a similar reputation as a dour man, but even he was taken aback when he returned to Kingsclere having rather unexpectedly won the Eclipse Stakes for the Duke, then about the most valuable race in England, to find him sitting under a tree reading a book. On being told the news of his victory the Duke replied: 'I am not interested, he is only moderate.'

The best horse the Duke owned was Ormonde, a son of Bend Or, who was undefeated in fifteen starts. Before the 1886 Two Thousand Guineas it was generally thought that Ormonde would be beaten by Minting, another unbeaten colt trained by Matthew Dawson. A few days before the race Dawson met Porter and Ormonde on the Heath at Newmarket. Dawson inspected Ormonde with care:

'Is he a good horse, John?' asked Dawson.

'Yes.'

'Is he a very good horse?'

'Yes.'

Then, in broad Scottish, 'Is he a dommed guid horse?'

'Yes.'

'Well then, you'll finish second!'[2]

Ormonde beat Minting comfortably, with the rest of the field a distance away, whereupon Dawson retired to bed for a week. The pair met again in the Hardwick Stakes at Royal Ascot the following year, and though Ormonde was extended on this occasion he again defeated Minting. The Duke of Westminster was very excited by this and he led his horse out of the winner's enclosure, twice around the paddock, and then out on to the course towards the stables; he seemed to be unwilling to let go of the leading rein. This was the year of Queen Victoria's Jubilee, and as his contribution to the festivities the Duke gave a reception for Ormonde at Grosvenor House in Park Lane. Ormonde came up from Kingsclere to Waterloo, and was then walked to Park Lane amid great acclamation. Waiting for him there were the Prince and Princess of Wales, four Kings, two Queens, various Princes and Princesses, and presumably many others. Ormonde took this all in, and according to his trainer enjoyed eating the sugar and flowers he was offered by the ladies.

Those racing men, like George Lambton in his autobiography *Men and Horses I Have Known*, who looked back to the 1880s with nostalgia in the years after the First World War were not simply exalting the jockeys and horses they had witnessed in their youth. The transformation of the racing world was such that there was little point comparing St Simon and Ormonde with the horses of the 1920s, or Archer with Steve Donoghue. The passing of anti-betting laws in the State of New York towards the end of the nineteenth century convinced many American owners, trainers, and jockeys that it was worth trying their luck in England, and by the turn of the century there was a large American community in Newmarket.

The successes of trainers like Andrew Joyner and J. Higgins, and jockeys like Tod Sloan and Danny Maher, drastically changed the techniques of their trades. The traditional jockey's seat was similar to that used by any proficient huntsman, sitting upright in the saddle with long stirrup leathers. Though Tod Sloan was not the first to ride in England in the modern style, crouched up over the neck and thus allowing the horse greater freedom of movement, his feat of winning twenty-one of the forty-eight races in which he rode in 1897 convinced the most sceptical of observers of the advantages of the style. By the turn of the century almost every English jockey had adopted the American style. The derivation of this style is uncertain, but it seems to have been an imitation of the seat adopted by Negro stable lads when riding exercise bareback. For those who could remember the elegance of Archer, the new style was never more than an unsightly necessity.

The American trainers proved conclusively that the racehorse did not necessarily benefit from being sweated, or from being kept in draughtless warm stables. They also managed to convince a few Englishmen that the stop-watch and scales for weighing horses were useful guides for any trainer, however experienced he might be at judging a horse's condition with his eye. What the English racing fraternity objected to, and what many still refuse to accept today, was the idea that the traditional skills of horsemanship are not as applicable to the racing world as they are to the hunting field. To those who have learnt to ride by following a pack of hounds, the style of a modern jockey is not only inelegant but also impractical, as such short stirrup leathers preclude the use of the legs for balancing and steering. Similarly if a man cannot tell if a horse is fit by looking at it, and is unable to produce a horse in such a condition without using a stop-watch, then he should not be looking after horses. To those, however, who have no pretensions to horsemanship, the modern seat appears to be effective as well as exciting to watch, and it is the occasional amateur who rides sitting upright who seems ridiculous in silks on the racecourse.

Such innovations altered the pattern of racing. Whereas before jockeys concentrated upon beating each other, trying to outwit their opponents by delaying their challenge until the last moment, or by pretending to be riding hard when in fact going easily, they now tried to cover the course in the shortest possible time. The earlier model of seat did not necessarily entail crawling until the last few furlongs; nor did the new one mean riding flat out from start to finish; but the Americans' judgement of pace meant that races were likely to be run in a shorter time. From riding exercise gallops against a stop-watch, American jockeys learnt how to gauge the speed at which a race was run, and thus to maintain a more even pace throughout a long distance race. The English model of jockeyship had evolved at a time when the most important races were matches and the psychological side of the contest was of great importance. Such changes made any comparison between Ormonde and Coronach, who won the Derby forty years later, tenuous as the racing mode and the style of their victories were so different.

The attitudes and objectives of those in the racing world were also beginning to change. In the 1880s racing could still be characterized as a contest between knowledgeable men. Those who did not have the funds to run breeding operations on the same scale as Lord Falmouth or the Duke of Westminster could buy good racing stock at moderate prices and hope to rely on betting to pay for their indulgence. The Duke of Westminster himself was an accomplished horseman, quite up to riding Ormonde in a gallop even though he was over sixty at the time. Yet racing appealed to many who had not the same founding in the lore of the horse, and as a consequence the value of bloodstock began to rise. In 1890 Baron Hirsch, a financier and friend of the Prince of Wales, caused a sensation when he gave 5,500 guineas for a yearling filly that had been bred by the Royal Stud. A contemporary observer reported:

We do like to see people spend money and if we think they are spending it rather foolishly, why, we cheer all the louder. . . . No one pre-
tends that when Baron Hirsch gave that extravagant price he was giving the value of the flesh, blood and bones that he was purchasing.

It turned out that 5,500 guineas was considerably less than the
flesh, blood, and bones of La Flèche, as the filly was named, was
worth, for she won the One Thousand Guineas, the Oaks, and the
St Leger, and was sold as a broodmare for 12,600 guineas.

Racing was becoming an entertainment rather than a sport, as was
shown by the changing status of trainers. For much of the
nineteenth century, training grooms were expected to wear livery
and attend race meetings in high hats, attired as any other household
servants. Matthew Dawson and John Porter were two of the first
trainers to run public stables, that is to own their own premises and
accept horses from whomever they wished. They both began their
careers in the employment of one patron but succeeded in establish-
ing sufficient reputations to set up on their own. This important
change in status was a reflection of the new money in racing. As
more people wanted to own good racehorses, those who were skilled in the art of training horses were able to charge higher fees, and
the range of services they offered broadened when their clients
ceased to be made up entirely of those who were horsemen themselves. Trainers took on the responsibility of planning the programmes of their charges and advising their clients at the bloodstock
sales. If it was still considered eccentric for a gentleman to become a
trainer, trainers were accepted socially on the racecourse, if not over
the dinner table.

Matthew Dawson is remembered today in connection with Lord
Falmouth, but he was never less than completely in charge of his stable. Lord Falmouth once ventured to advise a jockey as to how to
ride one of his horses and was promptly told by Dawson to remove
all his horses from the stable. It was only after Falmouth had
apologized and asked Dawson's brother to intervene on his behalf
that his horses were allowed back to Dawson's Heath House Stables
in Newmarket. Lord Falmouth remained a friend of Dawson's until
his death in 1889, and was frequently to be seen on the Heath with
the trainer watching the horses do their work. Dawson himself
retired in 1886 and moved from Newmarket to the nearby village of

Exning where he began to train again on a small scale at the request of another friend, the fifth Earl of Rosebery, for whom he trained two Derby winners.

Dawson was the first trainer to be accepted as a companion by the leading turf figures of the day, whether or not he actually worked for them. He retained his Scottish accent and partiality for whisky until the end of his life in 1898; the end having been hastened by a chill he caught through not wanting to cut short a conversation with the Prince of Wales on the Heath one cold morning. Besides his superlative record as a trainer, he trained six winners of the Derby and won twenty-eight classic races in total. He was also something of a poet.

John Porter, Dawson's contemporary, started training at the age of twenty-five in the employment of Sir Joseph Hawley Bt, on a salary of £100. On Hawley's death in 1875 he was given the option of buying the Kingsclere Stables, which he never had difficulty in filling. Most of his important successes were for the Duke of Westminster, Lord Aldington, and Sir Frederick Johnstone, though he also trained the horses of the Prince of Wales and Baron Hirsch for a time.

The Prince of Wales had his first winner on the flat in 1885, having become involved with racing at a late age due to the disapproval of his mother. That same year John Porter bought him Perdita as a broodmare for 900 guineas. Perdita's three sons, Persimmon, Diamond Jubilee, and Florizel II, earned him about £250,000 in prize money and stud fees, so he was probably one of the few people to have made money through owning racehorses. Persimmon won the 1896 Derby amid unprecedented scenes of jubilation, having come again in the last few yards to beat the odds-on favourite, St Frusquin, by a head. The very same head was preserved and is now on display in the National Horseracing Museum. His full brother Diamond Jubilee – they were both by St Simon – won the Triple Crown in 1900, but was a foul-tempered and at times savage horse. He was sold to an Argentinian breeder for £21,500 and was a great success as a stallion there until his death in 1923. Porter did not share in these triumphs, as the Prince's horses were moved to Richard Marsh's Newmarket stables in 1892.

Though it would have been impossible not to respect Porter's skill with horses it seems that those who enjoyed witticisms and had a sense of fun found him a difficult man to deal with. As Lord Marcus Beresford, the Prince of Wales's racing manager, had just such a reputation it was probably for this reason that Marsh was given the position of Royal trainer. Richard Marsh was in fact a public trainer, but it would be difficult to gather this from reading his autobiography.[3] He writes of the Prince of Wales and Lord Marcus Beresford with reverence. As an example of Lord Beresford's humour he cites his attempt to sell Perier, an exceptionally good-looking horse but a perfectly useless one, to some Frenchmen:

'There, monsieur, is a horse after your own heart. He is of good colour, he is sound and he has splendid bone, and he certainly should have won the Derby.'

'Why didn't he win the Derby?'

'Well, at a most critical part of the race six or seven others passed him and he lost.'

The excitement of his yearly visit to Sandringham, when he was allowed to watch the Royal party and their guests shooting and given a personal tour of the stud by his Royal master, never seems to have palled for Marsh. For his part he did his utmost to please his employer, whether it was building a platform from which the Royal party could watch his gallops, or training three Derby winners for him. He writes of his charges with a similar reverence: 'The racehorse is very much like a human being. His temperature is the same and so is his temperament, if I may put it so. The higher the horse's breeding the more he must be studied.' For him the difficulty of training was not in getting your horses fit but in persuading them to do their best, and for this he felt it was necessary to know them as individuals:

> The training outside the stable is just common sense and instinct to do the right thing at the right time. . . . The supreme racehorse is the one of supreme nervous energy and vitality, which must be nurtured and never sapped . . . feeding wins more races than actual training on the gallops.

Marsh also considered the feeding of his owners to be important, for when the Prince of Wales partook of luncheon at Egerton House, he would employ the head chef of the Savoy for the day. Marsh's loyalty to the Royal Family was repaid by their loyalty to

him, and he trained for King George V from 1909 until his retirement in 1924.

After he had come to the throne, King Edward VII won the
Derby for the third time, his colt Minoru winning in 1909. Like
many who do not understand the luck involved in owning
racehorses, Edward VII had become disillusioned when for seven
years he had nothing but moderate horses. When he was on the
point of giving up he was persuaded by Colonel Hall Walker to lease
some of his yearlings, including Minoru. Colonel Hall Walker came
from a wealthy family of Liverpool brewers, and had dedicated his
entire life to the study of the breeding of the thoroughbred. He was
not particularly liked as a result of his firm conviction that he knew
more about breeding and racing than anyone else. He would position himself on the rails of the paddock before a big race and
announce to everyone within earshot that the favourite was lame in
a place that no one else had heard of, that another contender had a
quite impossible sire, and that a third was obviously unfit. These
were not his opinions, they were 'facts' that were clear to anyone
who knew anything about racing, which of course no one other than
Colonel Hall Walker did.

Hall Walker never made any important decision without referring
to his own horoscope, or that of the horse in question. He insisted
upon knowing the exact time and place that each of his foals was
born so that he could construct their horoscopes, and determine the
fortune that awaited them. This occasionally led to disasters. On
one occasion he had a horse running at Royal Ascot that his trainer
considered to be a certainty but Hall Walker knew had no chance as
the stars were all wrong, and he told the King so when he inquired
about the horse's chance. The trainer proved to be correct, for the
horse won easily. The King was so angry, presumably due to having
backed another horse, that he found Hall Walker, thanked him for
his advice, and informed him that he intended never to consult him
again.

When Minoru was born at Hall Walker's stud in Ireland, the stars
were so perfect that it was beyond question he would win the
Derby. Being a loyal subject, he persuaded the King to lease Minoru. He was proved correct after a bizarre sequence of events; the
favourite, an American colt called Sir Martins, crossed his legs and
fell shortly after entering the straight, thus hampering every other

runner except for Minoru. The jockey of Bayardo, proved by later events to be by far the best horse in the race, claimed he lost at least sixteen lengths in the incident. After this mêlée Minoru only held on to win by a head that was so short that most of those present were of the opinion that the judge was a particularly loyal subject too. Minoru was later exported to Russia and shot in the aftermath of the Revolution as a consequence of his aristocratic connections.

In 1916 Colonel Hall Walker made a gift of all his thoroughbreds to the nation and sold his Irish stud and his training establishment at Russley Park in Wiltshire to the government. In recognition of this act he was created Lord Wavertree and elected to the Jockey Club.

During the Edwardian era racing became particularly dissipated. Many of the American owners who came over to England were somewhat disreputable, or at least not the sort of men the English were accustomed to see leading in the winners of their great races. There were numerous scandals, with the American jockeys Tod Sloan and Lester Reiff being banished from English racecourses for fixing races in order to ensure their success at gambling. Many American trainers owed their success more to skill at administering cocaine to their charges than to any understanding of the horse. Doping was not a problem that the authorities had had to deal with before, and it was only after George Lambton had demonstrated the complete transformation that cocaine could bring about in a roguish horse that it was made an offence to use such drugs. As with people, the short-term effects of cocaine on a horse may be palatable but any animal that is regularly doped is likely to break down either physically or mentally.

This was a time when there was a self-conscious 'sporting set', many of them permanently in debt, borrowing from one moneylender in order to pay back another. All were preoccupied with gambling and were regularly to be seen spending their winnings in smart London restaurants: Romano's and Princes were the most favoured.

One of the first gentlemen trainers, Peter Purcell Gilpin, set himself up as a trainer in Newmarket with the proceeds of a gamble on his filly Clarehaven in the 1900 Cesarewitch, building a stable that he named in her honour. He won another fortune when Major Eustace Loder's colt Spearmint won the 1906 Derby. Spearmint had been a moderate two-year-old, but there was a rumour the following spring that he had improved considerably. When Gilpin was planning to try Spearmint for the Derby the touts were waiting outside Clarehaven at four o'clock in the morning. So he took up the railings at the back of the yard, led his horses out across Lord Derby's land, and worked them on Lord Derby's private gallops. To ensure that he got the stable money on before the bookmakers heard of the gallop, he then locked all the jockeys who had ridden in the trial in the house in which they were breakfasting. Spearmint won the Derby at six to one, though Gilpin had taken twenty to one for his money.

One of the American owners who was never accepted by the establishment was Richard 'Boss' Crocker. Crocker was born in Ireland but went to the United States when young. There he went into local government and ended up as a powerful figure in New York City politics. He was forced to give up his lucrative and responsible post when Theodore Roosevelt set up a commission to inquire into alleged irregularities. Crocker himself denied that he ever made a dishonest dollar, declaring that he may have been a fool but never a knave. He arrived in England with the idea that American horses were superior to English ones, and he brought with him a string of horses with the intention of proving his point. He had bought them from a gentleman who used to travel across the country with his horses and a considerable harem. The horses may have won many races, but the harem did not go down well with the racing authorities: he was asked to choose between the two. He chose to remain loyal to his women, and his horses came to England with Crocker.

Unfortunately for Crocker the horses were either moderate or played out through having been regularly doped. It was not until he bought a stud in Ireland and raised his own stock that he had any great success. His Derby winner Orby was by the Duke of Westminster's stallion Orme, though he was out of an American mare.

Crocker's wife, who was reputed to be of Cherokee descent, was keen to be a social success and used to invite the local gentry and dignitaries to tea at their Berkshire house. The only part that Crocker played in these occasions was to put his head around the door with a cigar in the side of his mouth, nod genially to the thirty or forty guests, and say: 'How do, folks!' before disappearing again. His cigars became a well-known feature of race meetings; he used to have them sent to him from Havana 10,000 at a time, each with a gorgeous band on which 'Boss Crocker' could be seen from the furlong pole.

Crocker's love of four-legged champions led him to buy a bulldog that he considered to be the best of the breed for £800. He took 'Rodney Stone' around the country, winning many prizes. When he was finally beaten, determined not to be denied this pleasure he bought the dog that beat him for £1,000. His first English trainer, Charles Morton, writes of him with a humorous respect,[4] but soon came to realize the impossibility of training for someone with such decided views on the subject.

Morton himself was more tolerant of his owners than many in his profession, for before settling down to work for Jack Joel he trained for Robert Standish Sievier. Sievier was the perfect model of an Edwardian rake. According to his autobiography he was born in a hansom cab. He certainly did not inherit any money, and though he spent large quantities he cannot be said ever to have been rich; however much money he had, he was always prepared to stake the lot on a horse. Sievier was once at Sandown with his favourite daughter, Gogo. She was seen running up to him on the lawn:

'Daddy, Daddy! I've just won five shillings.'

'Have you, darling?' he replied. 'I have just lost five thousand pounds.'

When things were going well, Sievier could be extravagant. Morton recalls lunching with him at Romanov's; on tasting his wine he called Romanov over and asked him if he had a lot of it. On hearing that he had a large supply he bought fifty dozen bottles, which were finished within three weeks. For a time he ran a newspaper called *The Winning Post*, a scurrilous forerunner of *Private Eye*'s 'Colonel Mad' column. He was also involved in some famous law suits: he was acquitted of blackmailing Jack Joel, but ruined by a libel suit he brought against Richard Wotton, who had written that he had been wrongfully acquitted on the earlier charge. Like many who endeavour to expose corruption for the 'public benefit', Sievier was hypocritical and self-righteous. His last fling was in 1922 when he borrowed all he could in order to back Monarch for the Royal Hunt Cup. When the horse was beaten he was forced to sell his stables and newspaper, and give up his position as a public figure.

Horse-racing continued in England throughout the First World War, though on a limited scale, with all the important races being run at Newmarket. This was largely the result of Lord Durham's efforts to convince the government that it was crucial that every equine generation be tested on the racecourse in order to select those to be used as stallions. To show that his only interest in this matter was the lasting benefit of the breed, Lord Durham made a point of not setting foot on a racecourse for the duration of the war.

By 1914 horse-racing had already ceased to be the sport it was once held to be. Social pressures and the innovations that followed the Americans to Newmarket had already started movement towards an entertainment industry. Racing had never had such a popular following. A feature of the last five pre-war seasons that attracted particular interest was the rivalry between the Australian jockey Frank Wotton, who became champion at the age of sixteen in 1909, and the American Danny Maher, who regained the title in 1913. The pre-war years also saw the foundation of the two studs that were to be prominent in the coming decades: though Lord Astor and Lord Derby may have aspired to race in the traditional manner, they both made concessions to the changing times and had a decisive influence on the future development of the thoroughbred and the pattern of horse-racing.

2

Tradition and Change

If it were not for the fact that he was an American who came into racing purely by chance, Waldorf Astor could be said to be the perfect example of the traditional racing patron. Only his sophistication and broad range of interests truly differentiated him from someone like the Duke of Portland. He was born into an immensely wealthy family that owned large chunks of New York. Whilst he was a boy his father decided to settle in England, and it was as an undergraduate at Oxford that he first became interested in horses. He bought himself a five-year-old mare called Conjure with the idea of breeding hunters and point-to-pointers from her. To his surprise and delight, she proceeded to produce good class racehorses, and in 1910 her daughter Winkipop won the One Thousand Guineas. After this piece of fortune he bought himself another twelve mares with the idea of setting up a stud at Cliveden, the family house in Berkshire. His son, the Hon. Sir John Astor, says that he considered the breeding of racehorses to be the perfect hobby, like producing roses or breeding labradors; it was absorbing and inexpensive.

Of Astor's original mares, only the first two were any good: Popinjay, whom he bought from the fifth Earl of Rosebery for 1,000 guineas; and Maid of Mist, whom together with her filly foal cost him 11,500 guineas at public auction in 1911. From 1917 to 1929 he was remarkably successful with the decendants of these three mares – his good luck in the Oaks, which he won five times, being balanced by bad luck in the Derby, in which his horses came second five times in seven years. After buying his original mares he bred all his horses at the Cliveden Stud, whose operations he closely supervised. Astor would make a meticulous study of any stallion before sending one of his mares to him, taking the exact measurements of his head, ears, etc. and then trying to match the mare's confirmation with that of her prospective mate. Some of the more fashionable American bloodstock agents today can be seen approaching yearlings at the Keeneland Sales with tape measures and notebook at the ready, but in Astor's day this was considered to be eccentric behaviour.

Retiring from the turf in 1950, Lord Astor divided his horses between his eldest and youngest sons, W.W. and J.J. Astor. The last good horse he owned was the 1945 Two Thousand Guineas winner Court Martial. Racing was nothing more than a sport to Astor, and its interest for him lay mainly in his stud. He never had a bet and he sold most of his colts after their racing careers. This was unusual, as those who had the good fortune to breed a top class colt were then expected to retain them as stallions for their own stud. Astor preferred to use the best outside stallions available rather than relying upon his own. This may have been a mistake, for among the colts he sold were St Germans, who became a champion sire in the United States, and Saltash, who did the same in Australia.

On a day when an Astor horse was fancied, he, his trainer Alec Taylor, and his racing manager Gerald Deane would appear wearing a pink carnation to match the Astor colours of light blue with a pink sash and cap. Gerald Deane, who was also a partner of Tattersall's the bloodstock auctioneers, was an excitable man. After Astor's colt Buchan had been beaten when a short-priced favourite for the 1919 St Leger, Deane had to be restrained from attacking the jockey Joe Childs, whom he considered to have been responsible for the horse's defeat.

Alec Taylor, who trained in the Manton stables where Michael Dickinson will start his career as a flat trainer, made a considerable amount of money out of racing. As neither Lord Astor nor his other patrons, who included the first Lord Manton, Washington Singer, and Lady James Douglas, were interested in betting, his horses were never rushed and were given all the time they might need to come to their best. His stable lads were not shown the same consideration, being allowed out of Manton on only two weekends a year. On these occasions all the houses in Marlborough, the local town, would be locked and barred as 'the wild men' were coming down from the hills. Taylor inherited Manton from his father, 'grim old Alec' Taylor, and as well as passing on his skill with horses old Alec seems to have passed on some of the attributes that led him to be known as 'grim'. Alec Taylor never showed any interest in the luxuries that he could have well afforded; and when he died in 1943, sixteen years after handing over his stables to Joe Lawson, he left nearly £600,000. He was champion trainer for the seven consecutive seasons from 1917 to 1923 as well as on five other occasions, a record that explains why he was known as 'the wizard of Manton'.

Lord Astor's primary interest in life was politics. He was Conservative M.P. for Plymouth when in 1919 he inherited the title, which had been conferred on his father only two years before. He tried to renounce his peerage, but as the law then stood was unable to do so, and his wife Nancy Astor took over his seat, becoming the first female Member of Parliament. The 'Cliveden set', as the regular visitors to their house have since been called, were better known for their political, literary, and artistic talents than for interest in sport or racing. There are few who can afford to race in a similar style today, for as a hobby the breeding of racehorses has become considerably more expensive than the breeding of labradors. Astor, however, never had to worry about the expense – though shortly after the First World War when he was still paying American as well as British taxes he had a negative income, his cumulative tax rate being 110 per cent.

The seventeenth Earl of Derby was the most successful British owner-breeder ever. From 1908 when he succeeded to the title until his death in 1945 he owned the winners of over 1,000 races, including twenty classic races, and he was the leading owner in Britain on seven occasions. The horses he bred included stallions as influential as Phalaris, Pharos, and Hyperion, who could be said to have altered the course of the development of the thoroughbred; yet he had only around thirty horses in training each year. Lord Derby inspired the almost feudal loyalty that few peers now command. He would be cheered by the crowd when he arrived at Liverpool, his local racecourse, and his victories there were particularly popular.

During the 1923 General Election, Derby wrote to his trainer George Lambton saying that he was too busy to go racing as two of his sons, his son-in-law, and his brother were fighting Lancashire seats. It is unlikely that the electors of Lancashire would expect to be represented in Parliament by the family of the local Earl today. He played a considerable role in political life, being ambassador in Paris from 1918 to 1922, where his Englishness, carried to the extreme of not speaking French, was very popular in some circles, and holding the position of Secretary of State for War in Lloyd George's and Bonar Law's governments.

He bought a villa on the Riviera, which he named Sansovino after his first Derby winner, in order to escape the worst of the English winter – to the great annoyance of his children, who would have preferred to be in England hunting. Among his neighbours there was the Aga Khan, who, as a gesture of goodwill, used to send a crate of mangoes to Knowsley, Lord Derby's Lancashire home, every Christmas. Unfortunately the Stanley family were not as keen on mangoes as the Aga Khan was, and the arrival of the annual crate became a matter of exasperation.

The Stanley family had a long tradition of involvement in racing. It was at a party given by the twelfth Earl of Derby at his Epsom house, The Oaks, that the two Epsom classic races were planned in 1779. When the sixteenth Earl inherited the title from his elder brother in 1893 he decided to revive this interest. He refurbished the stud at Knowsley, which had been left empty for thirty years, and appointed George Lambton as his trainer, initially at Bedford Lodge in Newmarket, but he had the new Stanley House stables built and his string moved there in 1904. By the time of his death in 1908 his only notable success had been two victories in the Oaks, but the foundations had been laid, and his son, who had assisted him with the whole project, was able to maintain the existing arrangements with extraordinary success.

The seventeenth Earl's horses were, with the exception of the few he kept in France, all trained by a private trainer at Stanley House. He always retained a jockey, from whom he expected complete loyalty, though he was prepared to sack Tommy Weston without any explanation after ten years' service. Almost all his horses were bred at Knowsley or at the Stanley House Stud in Newmarket, and he never sold the superior colts that he produced, preferring to stand them at his own stud. Though a member of the Jockey Club he played little part in the administration of racing, occasionally intervening informally if he felt his interests were threatened.

Derby's views on racing were not thought of as progressive or radical. Yet despite the fact that his approach to racing was so traditional, the long-term influence of his racing programme was decidedly innovative. This was largely due to the fact he chose

George Lambton as his racing manager and trainer in 1893 and maintained their partnership for forty years. Derby was well informed about most aspects of racing but because of his other commitments he never had the opportunity to acquire the degree of expertise that a man like Lambton possessed; nor was he ever able to supervise the running of his stud and stables. As he was always ready to admit, he owed his success to the skills and advice of Lambton and his stud managers John Griffiths and Walter Alston.

George Lambton began training in 1882 after a bad fall at Sandown had ended a very successful career as an amateur jump jockey. His finances were in their usual rocky state, and only after his elder brother had guaranteed his overdraft was he able to set up in a small yard in Newmarket. It had been only a few years earlier that his brother, the third Earl of Durham, had in desperation arranged for him to go to Canada to take up a post with their uncle, who was then Governor General. The proposed journey was thwarted by George Lambton's arrest on the quayside at Liverpool on the instructions of the money-lender Sam Lewis. It later transpired that Lewis had approached Lambton's friend Lord Marcus Beresford and asked him if it was true that he was being sent against his wishes. The result of the meeting was that they arranged to have Lambton arrested and allowed to go free only once he had agreed not to leave the country.

A frequent visitor to Lewis's offices from the age of twenty, Lambton had bought his first racehorse for £150, despite not having a penny to his name. His subsequent friendship with Lewis was based not only upon the fact that the money-lender was fair in all his dealings, but also on Lambton's admiration for the methods Lewis used to redistribute his wealth. Besides being a regular at the casino in Monte Carlo, Lewis's wife always had a box at the opera and the best pair of carriage horses in London, which as Lambton pointed out was saying a great deal in those days.[1]

Lambton was the sort of Edwardian gentleman who considered money unimportant as long as there were money-lenders prepared to advance him the odd £1,000 for a couple of months. Shortly before his marriage in 1908, the Earl of Durham, having settled all his debts in London, asked him if there were any more outstanding. 'Oh,' he replied, 'I believe I also owe a few trifles to some locals in Newmarket.'[2] These trifles included a bill to one grocer that amounted to over £3,000.

It was as well for Lambton that Lord Stanley happened to be in the same house-party for Royal Ascot in 1892. Stanley told him that he hoped to revive his family's fortunes on the turf and asked him if he would consider training for him and his father. Lambton refused, saying he had not sufficient experience, but Stanley was determined and in 1893 Lambton took control of the Derby horses. It was not until 1924 that they achieved their primary aim, to repeat the family's solitary success – in the race to which they had given their name – achieved by the twelfth Earl in 1787. Sansovino's victory was greeted with great enthusiasm despite the pouring rain; for not only was Lord Derby popular with race-goers, but the colt started favourite. Indeed, Lambton and others connected with the stable landed a substantial gamble in the process.

Lord Stanley's determination must have been in part the result of a wish to have a trainer of similar social standing to himself. George Lambton was never thought of as an ordinary trainer: the fact that the brother of the Earl of Durham, the Duchess of Leeds, the Countess of Pembroke, Lady Robert Cecil, and Lady Anne Lambton chose to train racehorses was a matter for comment in the social press. When Lambton decided to marry Cicely Horner in 1908 the newspapers carried descriptions of him on the gallops in his flamboyant suits, the trousers of which were always creased at the sides, with his pekinese at his heels, the very picture of the dilettante trainer. Among the witnesses at the wedding were Prime Minister Asquith, Lord Derby, Lord Durham, and Lord Marcus Beresford. King Edward VII sent a personal letter of good wishes. After a short honeymoon the Lambtons moved into Stanley House, though due to Cicely's dislike of being so close to 'George's work' they soon moved to Mesnil Warren on the other side of the Bury road. It was typical of Lambton that when they decided to use some of his winnings from Sansovino's Derby to extend Mesnil Warren it was Sir Edwin Lutyens who was commissioned.

The first of the gentlemen trainers, Lambton inspired something akin to devotion from those who worked with him. When he finally left Stanley House, almost the entire staff moved with him; though it must have been obvious that his replacement, Colledge Leader, would always have better horses in his care than Lambton could hope for without Lord Derby's backing. Those who knew him remember him as perhaps an arrogant man, but above all as intelligent and capable. It was said more than once that if he had not been so fascinated by horses he could have been an excellent politician.

For such a man to become a trainer inevitably raised the prestige of his contemporaries and their profession. Not that he necessarily considered them to be his equals: it was rare for him to dine with his fellow trainers, and Lord Derby's jockeys were expected to stand up while he talked to them in his office. Such behaviour was not considered reactionary then, and he was widely respected. Richard Marsh wrote in his autobiography:

> I consider it has been a fortunate thing for the trainers of Newmarket that for so many years they should have had among them a gentleman like Mr. Lambton, who could always be relied upon in times of trouble or crisis to stand by them with his advice and example.[3]

Lambton's ambiguous relationship with Lord Derby occasionally led to difficulties. In 1919 Derby refused to have any of Lord Rosebery's horses at Stanley House, and was annoyed when Cicely Lambton wrote to him asking if he minded if they took one horse belonging to Giles Loder, a friend of hers. Derby replied with a letter that the Lambtons thought included a lecture on the relative positions of master and servant. After a period of antagonism they became friends again, though Loder's horse was never allowed into Stanley House. The fact that many of Lambton's friends were in the Jockey Club never stopped him from criticizing them if he thought fit. After the war he warned Lord Derby that the Jockey Club was completely out of touch with the general feeling of the racing world and he supported the numerous complaints about C. W. Marriott from his fellow Newmarket trainers.

Marriott was the Jockey Club's agent in Newmarket, and as such it was his responsibility to manage the town's gallops. He gained a reputation for being something of a pedant, fining the most grand of trainers for the most trivial of offences, and having no inclination to adapt any rule or custom to suit the circumstances. He is even supposed to have taught the gatemen at Newmarket to be as rude and aloof as himself. Lambton declared that Marriott 'would be far happier with soldiers, as the farm and the racehorses are of no interest to him';[4] and he asked Derby to lodge a complaint with the stewards on his behalf.

The success Lambton had as a trainer depended upon Lord Derby's stud, for which together with Walter Alston he was responsible. Alston was a specialist in the theoretical side of breeding, and would advise Lambton on the suitability of a prospective purchase's pedigree and the more likely outcomes of a particular mating. By 1910 when Swynford won the St Leger, the Derby studs had produced three classic winners in fifteen years: not a remarkable record, but better than most would achieve with only about twenty broodmares. Lambton always maintained that Swynford was the best horse he ever trained, arguing that he was never extended when he was at his peak. He was being prepared for the big autumn races as a four-year-old when he broke a fetlock joint during a gallop, one of the few incidents that caused the trainer to display any emotion in public. Swynford, in superb condition, was doing a half-speed gallop when he went out of sight behind a hut, for what should have been a few moments. He failed to reappear, and the next man to reach him found Lambton moved to tears by the sight of a magnificent creature hobbling forlornly on three legs. Surprisingly Swynford was saved and recovered to take up stud duties later.

Swynford apart, Lambton was not satisfied with the results of the breeding operation and he decided on a change of plan with the intention of introducing more toughness and speed. In 1913 they happened to breed Phalaris, who was a good middle-distance handicapper, and because there were no takers when Lord Derby tried to sell him during the First World War he was retained for stud. In 1920 he sired Pharos when mated with the daughter of a mare Lambton had bought with the intention of introducing toughness to the Derby horses. Pharos, besides finishing second in the Derby, became the foremost sire in Europe, the sire of Nearco, and the founder through him of the male line from which such as Northern Dancer and Nijinsky are descended. In fact almost all superior thoroughbreds today can be traced back to Phalaris in the main line, including such champions as Brigadier Gerard, Troy, and Shergar, all of whom are descended from Pharos's full brother Fairway. To breed from Phalaris, a horse who was at his best when racing over a distance short of a mile, was against the prevailing wisdom that to breed Derby winners it was necessary to use horses capable of staying the full distance of a mile and a half. In the forty years following 1910, Lord Derby's stud produced the winners of nineteen classic races, including three winners of the Derby, two of whom were descended from Gondolete, a mare Lambton bought from Colonel Hall Walker in 1912. When it is considered that at the same time Lambton helped the Aga Khan set up his stud it is not surprising that he was thought of as the foremost judge of a horse of his era.

In 1933 Lambton finally parted with Lord Derby, because Derby thought that at seventy-three the trainer was too old to be running a stable. In the last year of their partnership Lambton trained Hyperion to win the Derby and St Leger, though he was in such ill health that he was unable to go to Epsom and was forced to watch many of Hyperion's gallops from a chair on the balcony of Mesnil Warren that overlooks some of the training grounds at Newmarket. Unable to accept retirement, he set up a public stable and continued riding out every morning until a few weeks before his death. He had his last winner only two days before he died in 1945. He had given up briefly in 1926 when Frank Butters had taken over as trainer at Stanley House with Lambton staying on in the capacity of manager. Lambton seems to have been a difficult man to work with and the arrangement lasted only four years, with Butlers departing at the end of the 1930 season. They seem to have fallen out partly because Butters was not a first-class horseman himself, something Lambton considered any trainer should be, and partly because Lambton thought he gave the horses too much work, and was not as good a trainer as himself. The only assistant ever taken on at Stanley House, Alec Cottrill, did not last long either, as Lambton was convinced that he was hoping either to gain information with a view to betting, or to steal the Lambton secret of training horses. Lambton was never a dilettante trainer; as he says in his own book, training is a job that allows few holidays:

> With a large stable of horses there is very little time or leisure for other things; your horses occupy your thoughts, to the exclusion of everything else, and the man who is not always thinking about them is not usually much good at his job.[5]

He was, however, addicted to betting, and is said to have run Pharos in a small race at Newbury very soon after he had come second in the Derby because he was hard up and wanted something to bet on. Pharos, though not at his best, managed to scramble home.

Lambton was old fashioned in his loyalty, employing representatives of three generations of Rickabys as his stable jockey, and he always tried to help those whom he considered had served him well. Like many of his background, he liked to think that class was unimportant, and he possessed a touching faith in British society. He belonged to a generation to whom hunting and shooting were more than the social rituals they are today, being the means by which a man could display his daring, skill, and honour, those qualities most esteemed by gentlemen. Lambton even managed to admire Sir George Chetwynd, who was involved in a court case with his brother after the Earl of Durham had accused him of deliberately stopping his horses winning. Lambton wrote of the case: 'after watching him for days engaged in a struggle which meant practically life or death to him, his coolness, his pluck, and the staunch way he stuck to his jockey compelled my admiration'.[6]

During the Second World War there was much argument as to whether it was proper to continue racing while the country was at war. Pictures of large crowds at Newmarket for the substitute Derby brought indignant comments about the wastage of petrol and misuse of the railway system. Emmanuel Shinwell M.P. described racing in 1941 as 'An insane and unseemly spectacle'. In the same year George Lambton wrote in *Country Life*: 'Racing, there is no doubt, is the greatest factor in bringing together people of all classes. . . . Bismark's remark to Disraeli "so long as you keep your racing in England you will never have a revolution" should be remembered.' This does not seem to be a case of a member of a profession exalting its importance, but rather a comment indicative of those aspects of racing that Lambton most esteemed.

The following year Lord Derby gained his third and final success in his family's race when Watling Street won the substitute Derby run at Newmarket. The Earl was by this time seldom well enough to undertake the journeys necessary to see his horses run, and was content to leave that side of racing to his children and grandchildren. During the war, when they were both practically confined by their age to their houses, Derby and Lambton became friends again. They exchanged letters full of racing gossip and news of their children, who were fighting in various parts of the world. They were sentimental about the years when they had worked together, realizing that the racing world they had enjoyed would have disappeared by the time the sport got back to normal after the war. Lambton went as far as saying that he had no regrets at being so old, for he dreaded the thought of what life would be like for the so-called upper classes in ten years' time.

The extraordinary feature of both Lord Astor's Cliveden Stud and Lord Derby's Stanley House Stud was that such small enterprises, compared with the modern commercial studs, should have had such an influence on the thoroughbred. As a comparison one needs only look at the breeding programme of the Maktoum family today. Sheikh Mohammed plans to race around 100 horses of each generation, of which he hopes to breed about two thirds himself. Yet he and his advisers are aware that to ensure success at the highest level they will need to continue buying yearlings at the sales. Much of Lord Astor's success was the result of his three outstanding broodmares, so it is not surprising that he was unable to maintain the same level of excellence after their death. Yet through the sales of his outstanding colts, the Cliveden Stud blood was spread throughout the world. By breeding Phalaris and sending him some of his best mares, Lord Derby set in motion what Franco Varola, the Italian breeding specialist, has termed a revolution in the development of the thoroughbred: 'all these horses were bred at Stanley House Stud in England, thus confirming the historical trend that revolutions are actually engineered by people (or horses) of the opposite description to those whom they should theoretically benefit'.[7]

The Stanley House Stud was based upon a few outstanding broodmares, who were mated with the best British stallions of the day, most of whom were themselves owned and bred by Lord Derby. The most famous of these mares was Gondolette, who produced two classic winners herself; her daughter Serenissima produced another; and her daughter Selene produced Hyperion. Another was Scapa Flow, who produced the full brothers Pharos and Fairway, as well as the One Thousand Guineas winner Fair Isle. A hypothesis as to why no equine family today approaches such a level of sustained prepotency would be that such stallions as Phalaris broke down the rigid hierarchy that existed in the equine world at the time of the First World War. The achievements of the Cliveden Stud and the Stanley House Stud were possible only when the number of stallions and mares capable of producing classic winners was relatively small. Thus Lord Derby managed to acquire a higher proportion of such animals than anyone previously, and at the same time he introduced a new type of classic horse, rendering it impossible for anyone to repeat this feat.

What differentiated Phalaris's stock from those of his contemporaries was their speed. His best offspring, Fairway, Manna, and Pharos, were all very fast two-year-olds, yet contrary to the expectations of the breeding experts of the day they were all capable of winning over extended trips as three-year-olds. Fairway won the St Leger, run over a mile and three quarters, and Manna the Derby. This type of horse is well suited to a world where few have the time and money to wait for three or four years before receiving a return on their initial outlay. By the time of Lord Derby's death, Phalaris's blood had been spread throughout the world; Pharos's son Pharis was in France; Pharamond and Sickle, both sons of Phalaris and Selene, were highly successful stallions in the United States. At the time of Nearco's death in 1957 eighty of his sons were standing as stallions with representatives in almost every country with organized horse-racing. The international significance of Lord Derby's stud becomes even more evident when it is considered that sons of Hyperion became successful stallions in the United States, New Zealand, Australia, Argentina, and South Africa.

Lord Derby was an innovative influence on racing in many ways. Not only did he employ one of the first gentlemen trainers and introduce a strain of racehorse that ended the domination of a few established studs; he was also one of the first large-scale owner-breeders to try to make his racing profitable. He did not always manage to do so, partly as the result of the grand manner in which his racing was conducted: to maintain a private stable in Newmarket would be an unjustifiable expense for any owner today. The Earl was aware of this; indeed, the reason given for the termination of Frank Butters's contract was that he could not afford to employ both a racing manager and a trainer.

A financial deal led to the disagreement between Lord Derby and the Aga Khan, which resulted in the Aga Khan's being unable to send any of his mares to Hyperion. Shortly before the Second World War, Hyperion was standing at £400 – that is, the charge to a mare's owner for a mating – while the Aga Khan's Triple Crown winner Bahram was standing at £500. It was suggested that they exchange nomination, whereupon the Aga Khan said he was willing to agree as long as Lord Derby paid him the extra £100. Lord Derby was not pleased, and as the Aga Khan was never offered another nomination to Hyperion he was forced to buy any of his offspring that came on the market. Lord Derby's prediction that by the time racing had recovered from the Second World War those aspects that he most enjoyed would have disappeared was proved correct. What he cannot have foreseen was the extent to which he unwittingly set in motion those trends to which he would have objected: the end of the domination of a few small and private studs, and growing commercialism, with an expanding domestic and international market for potential broodmares and stallions.

3

The New Rich

Changes in the racing world are largely a reflection of broader social transformations. As a result of the interest in horse-racing shown by the new rich of the Edwardian and inter-war years, and because of the subsequent increase in the demand for racehorses, the intimations of change present in Lord Derby's breeding programme were swiftly realized and spread throughout the world. For every increase in the numbers of the affluent middle classes it is likely that some will choose to indulge in the luxury of owning racehorses; similarly a more general increase in welfare is likely to promote participation in horse-racing as an entertainment. After the First World War the former phenomenon was the more important, though there was also a boom in racecourse attendances and betting in the years immediately after the war. That this boom was not sustained was partly because those who ran racing did not see any need to encourage popular participation; but in any case, the feeling of economic exuberance was more psychological than an expression of altered circumstances.

The attraction of horse-racing for the new rich was not only that it appeared to be an establishment event, but also that it seemed to be the pastime of that part of the establishment that was flamboyant and glamorous. What differentiated those owners and prospective breeders who came into racing from the turn of the century onwards, from those within the existing tradition, was that for the newcomers to own good racehorses was only part of their purpose. To own racehorses, to talk of 'my trainer', or 'my jockey', was a way of achieving the sort of social prestige that no amount of money necessarily brings. It would be an oversimplification to say that this was the aim of all of those who succeeded in making a name for themselves on the turf, but it certainly played a part in determining the behaviour of some of those who wished to identify themselves with the aristocracy.

Many of the newcomers were far from being experts in the lore of the horse themselves, and were thus dependent on the advice of their trainer or other professionals. Many were also impatient for prestige, or for success before their money ran out, and were as interested in the early maturing horse or the fashionably bred yearling as in slowly building up a breeding operation over a number of years. The effect of this new interest in horse-racing was cumulative; for regardless of the nature of the existing sport, the newcomers added to it an attraction of their own: Solly and Jack Joel, and other Edwardian millionaires by choosing to own racehorses, increased the flamboyance and the glamour of the racing world, thus ensuring that successive generations of new rich would be drawn into it in the years to come. The first full racing season after the First World War was a perfect demonstration of the instant recognition that such newcomers could achieve. Not only did Lord Glanely win the Derby with Grand Parade, but seven of his horses were successful at Royal Ascot that same year.

William James Tatem had acquired a peerage by sending Lloyd George a cheque for £100,000 signed 'Glanely', after having had to work much harder for the money. He was a shipping clerk in Cardiff for seventeen years before buying a coastal steamer shortly before the Boer War; after the war he owned a fleet of cargo ships. He had his first winner in 1909, and from 1918 onwards devoted most of his energy towards racing. His extraordinary success in 1919 led him to go to the yearling sales full of confidence. That year he gave 11,500 guineas for Westward Ho, who turned out to be very moderate. The following year he broke the record price for a yearling again when he gave 14,500 guineas for Blue Ensign, who never won a race.

Lord Glanely was one of the first in a long line of men and women who have spent a considerable personal fortune on bloodstock with only meagre returns. People like Lord Glanely, the Gaekwar of Baroda, Lady Beaverbrook, and Captain Marcos Lemos were all ridiculed for a time, but eventually became accepted because it was recognized that they knew they were wasting money, but simply thought it a most enjoyable way to do so. They never felt the need to behave like Bond Street art dealers at an auction: Lady Beaverbrook used to walk to the front of the sales ring shortly before a lot came up that she wanted, making everyone turn over the page in the catalogue to see which yearling was destined to join Major Hern's stable.

Glanely was also well liked, partly because he dressed in what was thought to be an eccentric fashion. He only rarely wore a tie, and favoured light-coloured suits or flannels; he always wore a large panama and invariably carried a furled umbrella on his arm. The appearance of his portly figure and walrus moustache at the Doncaster Sales – Tattersall's used to hold their sales there – would be greeted by an inquiry from the rostrum as to which end he would care to bowl from. He was a patriotic man, his racing colours being a black jacket with a red, white, and blue belt and cap. His greatest personal sadness was that his wife was killed in a car crash shortly before his filly Rose of England won the Oaks. Lady Glanely had taken a liking to Rose of England after her husband had bought her as a yearling, and it was with tears coming down his cheeks that Lord Glanely led her and Gordon Richards into the winner's enclosure at Epsom. Richards remembers that the first thing he said to him was how her ladyship would have loved to have been there.[1]

In 1928 Lord Glanely took on Captain Hogg as his private trainer, after Gordon Richards had agreed to ride for Hogg during the coming season. He was thus one of the first men to retain Richards as his jockey. They parted at the end of the 1931 season when he tried to explain to Richards that due to the iniquitous rate of taxation he was unable to raise his retainer; he then rather spoiled his case by also telling him that he intended to spend £40,000 on yearlings that year, in the hope that this would persuade him to stay.

Glanely also had the dubious pleasure of owning Colombo. Colombo was spoken of as an outstanding horse after he had won his first nine races, including the Two Thousand Guineas. He then failed to win the 1934 Derby. More has been written about the 1934 Derby than about almost any other of its runnings. Steve Donoghue, who was aggrieved at not being given the mount on Colombo, claimed that he could have ridden the colt to win without coming off the bridle. Colombo, ridden by the Australian Rae Johnstone, who was having his first ride in the race, was interfered with by Donoghue's mount Medieval Knight coming round Tattenham Corner. He was left with a lot of ground to make up in the straight on Windsor Lad and Easton. After looking like making it he weakened to finish a length and a neck behind Windsor Lad and Easton. Some good judges thought Glanely was acting unfairly when he sacked Johnstone immediately afterwards.

In 1929 Glanely became the first self-made man to be elected into the Jockey Club. He had an unfortunate end, being killed in an air raid whilst staying at Weston-super-Mare. He was always known as 'Old Guts and Gaiters' by the racing public, probably a term of endearment.

If Lord Glanely was one of the more successful newcomers, in terms of both the races he won and the social recognition he gained, he was not the first to make a considerable impression on the racing scene. Among the first to do so were Solly and Jack Joel, who in their different ways made sure that they were noticed. Solly and Jack Joel's father Joel Joel was the proprietor of the King of Prussia, a pub in the East End of London. Their uncle, Barney Barneto, left England in 1873 to prospect for diamonds in South Africa, after he had failed to make a mark as a music-hall comedian. He arrived at Kimberley on foot, having had to walk the 600 miles from Cape Town, as he could not raise the price of a railway ticket. Yet, when De Beers Consolidated Mines was formed in 1884 it was Barneto who was the largest individual shareholder, even though Cecil Rhodes and his backers held a controlling interest in the company. The name De Beers was that of the brothers who had sold their farm for £6,000 in 1860 because they were fed up with the endless foreigners who invaded the area searching for diamonds. It turned out that the two mines later built on what had been their farm, the Kimberley mine and the De Beer mine, contained the majority of the world's diamonds.

Jack and Solly Joel, and their elder brother Woolf, went out to join their uncle and were given positions in the firm. As Kimberley became a more respectable town they diversified their interests, setting up breweries and insurance firms, and financing tours by London theatre companies. When Solly Joel returned to London in 1896 he was described in the press as the richest young man in the country; he was then only thirty-one. During a short stay he bought himself a Mayfair residence in Great Stanhope Street.

At this time Barneto was still the leading figure in De Beers Consolidated Mines, being along with Rhodes a director for life, but he was now an old man. He was returning to England with Solly Joel when he met his death. The official story is that Barneto and Joel were walking on deck after lunch discussing business when Barneto took leave of his senses and began climbing over the ship's rail. Joel, like a dutiful nephew, tried to stop him, but was unable to do so. The only witness was Fourth Officer W. T. Clifford, who said at the inquest that he had been asleep until he was woken by Joel's cries of 'Help! Help! Murder!' When he jumped to his feet he saw that Barneto was in the water. Although he immediately dived in, and managed to reach Barneto while he was still alive, the old man never regained consciousness. A verdict of death by misadventure was returned.

Shortly after this, Woolf Joel was shot dead in most mysterious circumstances. The man who shot him, who was known by the assumed title of Baron Von Veltheim, claimed he had been hired by Barneto to investigate a plot to overthrow the South African government. The result of these deaths was that Solly and Jack Joel took control of the many family business interests. Both brothers had owned racehorses in South Africa for some years, but at the turn of the century Jack Joel bought some horses in England, at the same time as taking control of the London end of their business. He was unable to return to South Africa, as he had jumped bail on a charge of illicit diamond buying.

Solly Joel remained based in South Africa for a time, giving dinner parties in Johannesburg at which his guests ate off gold plates and the tables were decorated with huge replicas of his mines made in solid gold; but he was soon looking for more competitive social fields. In 1903 he bought a 1,000-acre estate at Maiden Erlegh, near Reading, which he proceeded to refurbish. He made every effort to conform, becoming obsessed with doing things in the correct manner and meeting the right people. He sent his son Woolf to Eton. The scale of his flamboyance was such that it would have been impossible to describe him as another businessman turned country gentleman.

Joel acquired a passion for the paintings of George Morland and built up the second largest private collection of his work. He also seems to have enjoyed looking at Lady Hamilton, for he bought Romney's portrait of her as a Welsh girl and his study of her as 'Supplication', and a Gainsborough sketch of her head, to which he later added a portrait by Romney and another study of her as Ariadne. He bought finely bound editions of what were considered to be the classics of literature, but he was never observed reading anything more strenuous than the form book or his business papers. He built an enormous swimming pool of Italian marble at Maiden Erlegh, and then taught himself to swim. He was known to amuse himself by inviting large numbers of chorus girls, from one of the theatres he owned, down for the weekend. When they arrived he would suggest that they all went for a swim, and provided them with swimming costumes designed to disintegrate on contact with water.

It was at Maiden Erlegh that Joel gave his famous lunches on the Sunday before Royal Ascot, to which he would invite two or three hundred of the leading sporting and theatrical men of the time. Among them would be his business friends: Sir Abe Bailey, who had been in gaol with him after the Jameson raid;[2] Sir Alfred Butt, in partnership with whom he owned the Adelphi and Gaiety theatres and built the Empire Cinema in Leicester Square; Lord Dewar, with whom he smuggled alcohol into the United States during the years of Prohibition (Joel was said to receive two shillings and six pence for every case of whisky drunk in New York at the time). He would also invite his jockeys, his actors, and the press.

He was a great friend of Danny Maher's before the war, at one stage paying £500 a ride; later he befriended Steve Donoghue. Donoghue won a wartime Triple Crown on his colt Pommern, and went out to South Africa with Joel the following winter. Donoghue was unable to ride a winner during his stay until his patron bought the odds-on favourite of a race a few hours before it was run.

Also at Maiden Erlegh Solly Joel formed his stud, which he would inspect from the back of a white Egyptian donkey, for he hated walking. His valet used to remark that it had been a long time since he had had to do more than flick the dust from Mr Joel's boots.

When he was an old man, Joel used to complain that he had had a hard life, and that his greatest ordeal had been his ungrateful and selfish children. His eldest son Woolf became a wild socialite, giving lavish parties at the Ritz to which he would invite people who owed his father money, and then appear impersonating him. He gave his father a parrot to great him on his return to Great Stanhope Street from the office with: 'Hello, Solly! How's the market?' Solly Joel refused to pay his son's debts, and in the early 1920s Woolf was declared bankrupt. He was sent to work on a farm in Egypt, but he was found at the bottom of a companionway on the ship that was taking him there, dead with a large bruise on the back of his head.

His eldest daughter Doris married without his permission, whereupon he refused to talk to her. There was a short reconciliation when she produced a grandchild, but shortly afterwards they had a final row, after which he refused to acknowledge her existence. He changed the name of his yacht to *Eileen*, after his second daughter, destroying the plates and fittings on board that bore Doris's name and destroying her portraits. If he was ever asked about her he would declare he had no idea whom people were talking about, for he had no daughter called Doris. His second son Stanhope also married without permission, but he was not cut off completely for he provided grandchildren for Solly Joel to play with; Joel would not hesitate to ring Mrs Stanhope Joel at midnight and demand to see his grandchildren immediately.

After the split with Doris, Eileen took pride of place in his affections. He never allowed her a lapse in discipline, and even when he had been confined to bed by his doctors he would be up and waiting outside her room at five-thirty to ensure that she was on time for her morning ride. Eileen was a distinguished horsewoman, and once she had persuaded her father to allow her to ride astride, rather than sidesaddle, she won the Newmarket Town Plate, at the time the only race in which women were allowed to ride. That day Solly Joel placed what was for him a small bet on his daughter's horse and was furious to discover when he returned to collect his winnings that the bookmaker in question had disappeared. He asked a bystander if the man had known who he was and was told that the bookmaker certainly did, for on leaving he had said that Mr Joel might miss him but he would not miss the money.

Despite the enormous amount of time and money Joel spent trying to be accepted by the established sporting set, he was never taken completely seriously. His family suffered most from his pretensions, having to humour him by obeying his edicts. He did manage to become a well-known figure, however; when he drove from Great Stanhope Street to his office in the City in his peculiarly designed car, the police would hold up the traffic so that his progress was not impeded.

He never seems to have applied his mind to racing or breeding, being more interested initially in gambling, and later in the attention his horses brought him on the racecourse. He never appreciated that his racing could not be run like any other part of his business. He sacked his trainer Étienne de Mestre for replying to his request to show him his horses, after they had been bedded down for the night, by asking Joel if he thought he was running a circus. The only classic races Joel won were a wartime Triple Crown with Pommern – though his most famous victory was the 1906 Cambridgeshire with Polymelus, when he and his friends were supposed to have won in excess of £100,000. Numerous other good handicappers carried his colours of green and pink stripes with a pink cap, and he was the leading owner in 1922 and second to Lord Derby in 1924.

Joel made a last trip to South Africa in 1930 to attend a shareholders' meeting of De Beers Consolidated, but on his return to London he was obviously very sick. As he lay dying in Great Stanhope Street he gave strict instructions that whatever his condition his trainer, Walter Earl, was to be admitted as soon as he arrived. A last defiant gesture was to move to his Newmarket residence, Moulton Paddocks, in order to attend a race meeting. He never made it, dying on 22 May 1931. Joel's family continued to race after his death. His son Stanhope owned Busted, who won the King George VI and Queen Elizabeth II Stakes in 1967 in the pink and green, as well as Chamossaire, who won the St Leger. Mrs Stanhope Joel won the Oaks with Lupe in 1970, and Eileen Joel, who married after her father's death, won the St Leger with Athens Wood as Mrs John Rogerson.

Solly and Jack Joel always appeared to get on badly. If Jack ever interfered in his brother's family rows he would take the side of his children, or his estranged wife, against him. But if anyone attacked either brother in front of the other, each would make a point of defending the other. On the racecourse their rivalry was reasonably friendly. They had frequent matches between their horses, the most famous taking place in front of a large crowd at Hurst Park, when Jack Joel's champion sprinter Sundrige was surprisingly beaten by an inferior horse of Solly Joel's.

Jack took racing more seriously than his brother did, spending a considerable amount of money on his stud and employing Charles Morton as his private trainer. The best horse he bred was Sunstar, who won the Two Thousand Guineas and the Derby in 1911.

Sunstar broke down about a week before the Derby, but Joel and Morton decided it was worth patching him up to run, even though they both knew it would mean he would never run again. Sunstar was out of a mare called Doris, who had belonged to Solly; he was trying to get rid of her when Jack remarked that it was a pity to sell a mare named after his daughter. Solly replied that if he was so concerned he could have her. Morton worked for Jack Joel for twenty-three years, during which time the stable won eleven classic races, the last being Humorist's Derby in 1921. On Morton's retirement Joel lost interest, and by the time of his death in 1940 his Childwick Bury Stud was very run down, though for twenty years it had been the most successful private stud in the country.

Another newcomer to the racing world who became well known as a result of his character rather than his horses was James White. Jimmy White was a close friend of Solly Joel's. He may have made as much money as Joel, but he never acquired his friend's polish and ability to mix with any society. He also failed to die rich. The son of a bricklayer, White's wealth was founded in Lancashire cotton mills, but he branched out to be at one time or another either chairman or managing director of the Beecham Trust, the Dunlop Rubber Company, and the Bedford Estates. During the First World War he helped Joel run entertainments for American troops based in Britain, organizing steam-boat trips on the Thames near Henley, and visits to the theatre. Once, when late for a meeting with Joel and, because of the war, unable to find a cab, he hailed a bus and told the driver to go straight to Prince's Restaurant, thrusting fivers into the hands of anyone who complained.

White saw himself as the leader of the financial world. If his success was at another's expense then the competition only served to add interest to a deal. His main pursuit was money, how to make it, and how to spend it, and one of his greatest pleasures was displaying how much he had made. Racing appealed to him partly as a means of entertaining his friends, and also as a way of gaining prestige and showing that he had arrived. Perhaps its greatest thrill for him, however, was betting. He hoped to be able to say with conviction what Horatio Bottomley said in court when he was asked if he kept racehorses: 'No, they keep me.' One of his prized possessions was framed and placed on the wall of his office in the Strand – the result of a week's work, a cheque from his bookmaker for £50,000.

In the years immediately after the war White owned two of the best handicappers in the country in Ivanhoe and Irish Elegance, both of whom had been bought for him by his first trainer, Harry Cottrill. Irish Elegance won the 1918 July Cup; the following year he won the Royal Hunt Cup at Royal Ascot carrying nine stone and eleven pounds, including a ten-pound penalty for a win at Manchester a few days earlier. When White heard that he had been refused entry into the Royal Enclosure he threatened to withdraw the horse. He decided to run when someone pointed out that if the horse was withdrawn he would lose the vast sums he had already wagered on him. He was so confident on the morning of the race that he offered to sell Irish Elegance for a fiver if he lost.

White must have been a difficult man to train for. He thought he knew all there was to know about racing, and he liked his trainers to confirm this. When he moved his horses from Lambourn to Foxhill, near Swindon, by his country house King Edward Place, Martin Hartigan was installed as trainer.

During the racing season White would give lavish parties at King Edward Place. His guests would arrive in time for evening stables on Saturday, when they would be taken around the yard. All the lads wore spotless white jackets, while the horses were turned out to look their best, the yard was cleaned out, and fresh sawdust laid down all the passages. The following morning the horses would be paraded before exercise in a ring that had been built for the purpose outside the house. All the stable lads wore clothes made by the best military tailors in Swindon, riding breeches and shirts from Collins of Newmarket, and boots from Quants. After lunch there would be football matches between the Foxhill lads and those from nearby yards. For a time Gordon Richards was captain of the Foxhill team, having arrived there as a fifteen-year-old apprentice in 1920. White took these games seriously and wagered large sums on the result. He would always give rides to a lad who scored an important goal. Richards was awarded his first ride after scoring a penalty, and although the horse failed to win, he rode his first winner a few weeks later. After the football there would be a donkey derby between the stable lads and visiting actresses. (Like many of those interested in racing between the wars, White was equally fascinated by the theatre. In 1922 he bought Daly's Theatre. On meeting his friend Sir Harry Preston soon afterwards he justified his purchase by saying:

'It cost a quarter of a million but it was worth it. I've always wanted a theatre.')[3]

The entertainment at White's house-parties also included boxing matches. Until recently all stable lads were expected to box, and there is still a stable lads' boxing championship held annually in a London hotel. White's star entertainment was to match Jimmy Wilde, one of the greatest flyweights of all time, against lads four stone heavier than him – Wilde always won. The day would end with cockfights on the lawn of King Edward Place, or demonstrations of oddities like a monkey that killed rats with a hammer.

White could be generous to his employees. One former stable lad remembers that in his first week at Foxhill the whole staff were taken by a special train to London in order to see *Lady of the Rose* at Daly's. They had seats in the best boxes and were given a champagne party on stage afterwards.[4] The same man remembers that the food and accommodation were marvellous, so it is probably a tribute to Mrs Richards that Gordon Richards has written that the food was awful. Gordon Richards seems to have been overawed by Foxhill, which is not surprising, since the first motor car he ever sat in was the chauffeur-driven one that met him at Swindon on his arrival. He knew that not everyone as rich lived as he did, but promised himself that when he had as much money as Mr White he would be more careful with it. Richards left Foxhill in 1921 when Martin Hartigan left to take over his brother's yard upon his sudden death. White offered Hartigan £3,000 for Richards' indentures, and his refusal shows what a high opinion Hartigan had of his apprentice.

For many years White had a curious relationship with Steve Donoghue. It was never certain which one was manipulating the other, or whether they were friends. White was proud of the fact that Steve Donoghue, one of the most famous men in the country, was his stable jockey, his paid servant. Donoghue was a frequent guest at King Edward Place, but he was always as ready to talk to and advise the lads as he was to drink champagne with White. They both enjoyed betting. What would have been one of their best coups was foiled by Solly Joel. A horse of White's called Cloudbank came second in the 1925 Goodwood Stakes ridden by Donoghue. The race was run in a sea mist so thick that those on the stands were unable to see more than the last couple of furlongs. That night Donoghue told White that Cloudbank had had a very easy race, and advised him to run the horse again in the Goodwood Cup the following day, and to have £2,000 on him. White agreed to do this, and came down from London to watch the race. On his way from the paddock to the bookmaker's he met Solly Joel, who took him off to his box for a quick drink. By the time White emerged, Cloudbank had long since won the cup at ten to one.

There was something frantic, almost manic about Jimmy White. Something in his character drove him to do everything more flamboyantly than anyone else. Sidney Galtrey, who had no liking for him, described watching him at a dinner party:

> He surveyed his hearers as one does a panorama, keen to observe the impression he was creating. He had to impress them. His way of doing so was to monopolise the conversation in his immediate vicinity. He would listen when a sycophant with a special penchant had something specially palatable to say. Then back again to money. Always flirting with his chief god.[5]

By 1927 things were going wrong for White. He had an idea to buy numerous shares in British Controlled Oil Fields with the hope of pushing up the price, and then selling out to make a profit. To help his enterprise he wrote to many of his acquaintances telling them that in his opinion the share price of British Controlled Oil Fields was about to rise, and advising them to buy as soon as possible. Others with more long-term interest in the company recognized what was happening and attempted to inform people who were thinking of joining in the speculative rush of the true state of affairs; perhaps, also, some of White's acquaintances feared they were being conned. Whatever the reason there was a loss of confidence in White, and when he was asked to take up shares to the value of £1 million the banks refused him credit. That night he returned to King Edward Place and told his Chinese butler – most of his domestic staff were Chinese – to deliver a package containing some of his racing cups to his sons in Worthing. He then retired to his room. The butler broke down the door to his room the following afternoon when he failed to get any reply to his inquiries as to the state of his master's health. White was dead with a note beside him to the local doctor: 'Go easy with me old man, I am dead from prussic acid. No need to cut any deeper. Jimmy.'

Solly Joel seems to have had a genuine affection for White, and apparently could not understand why he had not asked him for a loan to help him through his difficulties. The reason became clearer the following year when it was disclosed that White had not paid income or super tax since 1921, and that at the time of his death he owed the Inland Revenue a figure in the region of £1,700,000.

Numerous other millionaires came into racing at this time. Though they were not all as colourful an addition to the scene as Solly Joel and Jimmy White, they all contributed to the transformation of the racing world. Among the more conservative was Lord Woolavington. After working as an agent for a firm of distillers he set up on his own as James Buchanan & Company. In 1918 he merged his company with Dewar & Sons, forming the largest whisky distilling concern in the country. He was seventy-three in the year he became Woolavington and owned his first Derby winner Captain Cuttle. Lord Woolavington was a quiet man, partial to the product that had brought him a fortune, and to talking about politics and pictures. The other passion of his life was the work of Dickens, and more than one acquaintance said that he would not have been out of place in one of the writer's novels. Sir Alfred Munnings recalls with pleasure his dinners with Woolavington while staying with him in order to paint his second Derby winner Coronach, adding that his parrot was unnerving.[6] Lord Woolavington had a chronic wheezy cough at this time; his parrot imitated it so well that it was difficult to be certain which of the two was coughing.

The immediate effect of the interest shown in racing by such men was not to raise the value of bloodstock – indeed, yearling prices were adversely affected by the general economic depression – but their involvement added to the attraction of horse-racing as a public spectacle, and transformed the roles of both jockeys and trainers. The independent stature that men like Matthew Dawson and Fred Archer had achieved earlier now became commonplace. The more successful jockeys were among the most famous men in the country, and the big trainers were in a position to reject any owner, secure in the knowledge that others would be only too pleased to take their place. The period between the wars was probably the time when leading jockeys and trainers were allowed the most independence. The hierarchical structure of racing had been loosened, and yet racing had not become purely a business. However, although these

changes benefited the top racing professionals, for many of the
trainers and jockeys of the period life went on much as before, as we
shall see.

4

Jockeys and Trainers

The period between the two world wars was the time of the 'playboy' jockey. Jockeys were no longer regarded by their employers as exalted servants, nor were they the dedicated professionals of today. Before the advent of evening meetings, and while trips to ride on the Continent at weekends were not obligatory, the life of a leading jockey was less hectic. As a result, they had more time to play up to their role as popular hero. Jockeys, like comedians and music-hall stars, were popular heroes not so much for what they did, but because the popular understanding of what they did was so limited. It was thought that the skills required for recognition and success could be inherent in any small boy; all that was needed, most people believed, was a lucky break and the consequent publicity. Just as many were lured into the entertainment world by stories of people from humble backgrounds becoming stars and appearing on London billboards within a few years, so many small boys went into racing stables in the hope of emulating the likes of Tommy Weston. The son of a wagon driver on the Yorkshire & Lancashire Railway, by the time he was twenty-one Weston was Lord Derby's stable jockey and a household name, having won the Derby on Sansovino.

The life of a jockey was, superficially, an attractive one. The leading jockeys bought themselves smart cars and country houses, they took on chauffeurs and servants, and they appeared in public only in well-cut suits or the smartest of breeches, with gleaming riding boots. They were often photographed with actresses or other 'sporting personalities', and appeared in films or took part in aeroplane races. This independence was conditional, for all jockeys relied upon the goodwill of the owners and trainers they rode for. Jimmy

White may have been flattered that Steve Donoghue chose to drink champagne with him, but there were still many owners who would have been horrified by the idea of drinking with their jockey.

Only those jockeys who became public figures were allowed to escape from the strict codes of discipline and loyalty most of the profession were expected to adhere to. The competition was so intense that few could afford to flout the wishes of those upon whom their livelihood depended. If jockeys today are more independent, the growth of other leisure industries has meant that horse-racing has lost the monopoly on glamour it once had.

Michael Beary was one of those jockeys who acquired a reputation as a womanizer and a socialite. He was frequently seen collecting well-known actresses from stage doors, in order to take them out to dinner, or dancing at three o'clock in the morning, dressed in white tie and tails, in a fashionable night-club. Beary managed to annoy his fellow jockeys with his tales of dancing with prominent owners' daughters at the Embassy Club, as they thought he was probably trying to take over their best rides. At the same time he annoyed the owners, who did not expect their daughters to dance with jockeys, or their jockeys to be drinking champagne at three o'clock in the morning before a big race. He was not often caught out, unlike Freddy Fox, who was seen drunk in a night-club at two o'clock in the morning, when he was due to ride a horse in the Oaks that afternoon – he was beaten a head, having ridden a most injudicious race.

For a time Beary was a great friend of Aly Khan's; teaching him the art of race riding, spending the winter hunting and socializing with him, and the racing season in London night-clubs. He had the distinction of having even less idea of the value of money than Steve Donoghue had, and an even greater ability to annoy those upon whose goodwill he relied. He was once suspended by the stewards, on the Tuesday of Royal Ascot, only to reappear on the Wednesday wearing his morning dress: he was escorted from the course.

Steve Donoghue had something of the same reputation. He never looked happier than when sitting in a casino with a girlfriend on one side and a bottle of pink champagne on the other. The difference between Beary and Donoghue was that no one found it possible to dislike Donoghue. He was selfish, self-indulgent, incapable of managing his own affairs, and convinced that he was beyond any rule or regulation, but charming and genuine in his desire to please.

Donoghue's break came when, after spells of riding in France and Ireland, he was offered the job of stable jockey to 'Atty' Persse in 1911. Two years later was the year of The Tetrarch; by the end of the 1913 season Donoghue was a well-known figure. The Tetrarch was an extraordinarily fast two-year-old, who was unbeaten in seven starts. The only occasion on which he was extended was at Sandown, when he almost fell at the start of a race; although he was tailed off at half-way he still managed to catch the leader in the last few yards and win by a neck. Known as the 'Spotted Wonder' due to his colour – grey with white patches – he captured the public's imagination. John Hislop cannot have been the only little boy who named his rocking horse after him. In 1914, at the age of thirty, Donoghue was champion jockey for the first time, a position he maintained until 1923. Unfortunately for him many of his victories were hollow as racing did not attract much public attention during the war.

After the war Donoghue became the popular hero he so wanted to be. A newspaper headline of the time declared, 'Steve mobbed by the demobbed!' He used to buy first-class railway tickets, only to arrive on the platform as the train was pulling out; he would jump on to the guard's van and stay there, happily chattering for the rest of the journey. Not only guards enjoyed his chatter; he was adored by the stable lads of the yards he worked for, always finding time to talk to them. After leaving Persse, as a result of his betting on stable information, he worked for Jimmy White, before becoming Lord Derby's stable jockey in 1921. George Lambton had the highest opinion of Donoghue as a jockey, writing: 'Stephen can find out more about what is left in his horse with his little finger than most men with their legs and whip.'

Donoghue lost the Stanley House job when he tried to get out of his commitments in order to ride Humorist in the 1921 Derby. Lord Derby, who was paying him a large salary to ride his horses, reluctantly agreed to let him, although he never employed him subsequently. The Earl thus joined the many influential owners who respected him as a jockey and found him amusing as a man, but felt it not worth their while to pay him for his loyalty.

Shortly before the 1922 Derby, Donoghue managed to persuade Lord Woolavington to give him the mount on Captain Cuttle; this angered his regular rider, Victor Smyth, but allowed Donoghue to ride his second successive Derby winner. In the aftermath of Captain Cuttle's victory, Woolavington took Donoghue on as his jockey. When it came to the 1923 Derby, he was expected to ride a horse of Woolavington's, trained by Peter Gilpin, but he managed again to evade his obligations and rode Papyrus to victory over Lord Derby's Pharos.

Fred Darling had no wish to take Donoghue on as his stable jockey, but he had no objection when Henry Morriss, a Shanghai bullion broker, arranged for him to ride his colt Manna in all his races in 1925. Darling insisted that whenever Donoghue was due to ride the colt at exercise, he spent the night before at Beckhampton, and he was woken two hours before the gallop was due to take place. Manna won both the Two Thousand Guineas and the Derby before breaking down.

In 1925 Donoghue was at the peak of his success, but not long after his last Derby victory he had a bad fall in France from which he never fully recovered. He did not ride another classic winner until 1937, the year of his retirement. That he retained his popularity with the public was largely due to his partnership with Brown Jack. Sir Harold Wernher bought Brown Jack as a potential hurdler and he proved to be a sound purchase. He won seven of his ten hurdle races, including the Champion Hurdle, before Donoghue suggested trying him on the flat. He proceeded to win the Goodwood, Doncaster, and Chester cups, the Ebor Handicap, and eight other races, as well as his famous six-timer in the Queen Alexandra Stakes at Royal Ascot: from 1929 to 1934, Steve Donoghue and Brown Jack won the race, their final appearance together being an occasion of unrestrained sentimentality.

After his retirement, at the age of ten, Brown Jack went to stay with Sir Alfred Munnings in order to have his portrait painted. During his visit, people came from all over East Anglia to see him, and he was cheered every day as he was led around the village for his morning exercise. He was a horse of character, occasionally crossing his legs, leaning against the railings, and going to sleep in the paddock.

Following their last success together, Donoghue flew to Paris to celebrate. At a party, during the early hours of Sunday morning, he was asked if he had a mount in the Grand Prix de Paris, the day's big race; he laughed and said that he was on holiday. Later that morning he was woken and told he had agreed to ride Admiral Drake in the Grand Prix. Despite his protestations of not being in a fit state to do anything, he allowed himself to be taken to the course. He won the race well, before opening more champagne to clear his head.

Donoghue seemed to acquire his taste for high life during the war years, which he spent in the company of men like Solly Joel and Jimmy White. Before the war he had led a respectable life in a country house near Stockbridge, with his first wife, the daughter of an Irish trainer. It was on the boat going out to South Africa with Joel that he met and began his affair with Eleanor Lady Torrington. Eleanor Souray had run away from home to go on the stage; having got a foot on the stage, she was successful enough in keeping it there to buy herself a few racehorses. She met Lord Torrington, when a horse of hers beat a horse of his at Ostend. They got married within a few weeks. Within a year Lord Torrington had been taken to court by a money-lender, and by the time he enlisted in 1914 the marriage was finished.

In 1917 Donoghue sold his Stockbridge home and moved to London. He became extremely dapper, wearing suits, shirts, and shoes especially made for him, and taking on his own valet and maid. Later that year he divorced his wife. In 1919 Lady Torrington bought Elston House, at Shrewton; the property included a stud and a racing stable, in which she installed her horses and a head lad – in whose name the training permit was taken out, since it was against the rules of racing for a woman to train racehorses. For the next ten years, Donoghue and Lady Torrington ran the stable together. The best horse they looked after was Embargo, who won the Irish Two Thousand Guineas and Derby, and the City and Suburban Handicap, for the Maharajah of Rajpipla.

Everywhere Donoghue went, Lady Torrington was there too. It was she who picked him up after his Paris fall, just in time to stop officials giving him an anaesthetic, to which he was allergic. She accompanied him on his trip to the United States, to ride Papyrus; she arranged for him to sell his life story to the *Daily Express* for £4,000, and no doubt she helped him land the hero's role in the film *Riding for a King*.

Sir Alfred Munnings recalls staying at Elston House and being entertained by Donoghue singing to Lady Torrington's piano playing.[1] This was shortly after Humorist's Derby. Munnings remembers arriving at Donoghue's flat – above the fishing tackle shop in Pall Mall – to find him, his valet, and his maid turning the place upside down; Donoghue had lost a cheque for £2,000 that Jack Joel had given him as a present. On the way to Newbury races, the couple's car was greeted by shouts of 'Come on, Steve!' as he was recognized by other race-goers.

Lady Torrington shared Donoghue's addiction to gambling, a harrowing moment being Papyrus's Derby, when they both had far more on him than they could afford to lose. As they came round Tattenham Corner, Donoghue went for home stealing a few lengths lead, but two furlongs out Pharos came alongside going easily; Pharos went ahead a furlong and a half out, but just failed to last home – Donoghue and Papyrus coming again to beat him by a length. Lady Torrington was the only lady present at the party Donoghue gave at Grafton's Galleries that night. It ended at dawn, with Donoghue being pulled around the dance floor on a wooden horse by Lady Torrington and the Earl of Lonsdale. George Lambton was so shocked by the newspaper reports that he suggested jockeys should not be allowed to celebrate until the end of the flat racing season.

By 1928 things were not going well for Donoghue or Elston House. He was now forty-four and past his best as a jockey, but unable to retire because he needed the money. In November of that year he was declared bankrupt with debts of over £30,000. His affair with Lady Torrington was over, and in March 1929 he married an American dancer, Ethel Finn. In 1930, Lady Torrington too was declared bankrupt and in December 1931 she took her own life, after the failure of a night-club venture. She left what remained of her property to Donoghue's children, having recently changed her will to remove his name. Although he rode Exhibitionist to win the One Thousand Guineas and the Oaks in his final season as a jockey, for most of the last ten years he was riding he was only moderately successful. For a time he was stable jockey to Basil Jarvis, though Jarvis gave him up after spending the whole of one evening trying to track him down in order to ask him to ride two horses at Lingfield the following day. He caught up with him in the Paris Ritz and persuaded him to come back. Arriving half asleep, the jockey got caught napping on the first and never showed on the second. Donoghue died in 1945, and his home town, Warrington, went into mourning.

Another jockey to achieve a degree of independence was Charlie Smirke. He was retained intermittently by the Aga Khan for thirty years, but it was never completely clear who was the patron and who the client. He started riding for the Aga Khan again in 1949, after Aly Khan had come up to him on the racecourse, put his arm around him, and announced: 'My father and I are missing you so much, Charlie. Racing isn't nearly the fun that it used to be.'

Smirke was apprenticed to Stanley Wootton in Epsom. Wootton was well known as a coach of young jockeys, his stable being referred to as 'Wootton's academy.' As well as maintaining strict discipline, he tried to impress upon his boys the importance of confidence, cleanliness, and obedience. Smirke seems to have always possessed a high degree of confidence; whilst he was still an apprentice he and Wootton were called in front of the stewards to give evidence at an enquiry, Wootton reprimanded him afterwards, saying: 'You shouldn't say "Coo! What a whopper!" when a senior jockey is stating his case.' Later, Smirke shocked the Aga Khan by replying to his casual question, in the paddock before the 1927 Ascot Gold Cup, as to what he would like as a present were he to win: 'An all-weather, three-and-a-half-litre Bentley.'[2]

In 1928 Smirke's career was cut dead when he was warned off, for allegedly pulling a horse called Welcome Gift, the odds-on favourite, at Gatwick. Any person 'warned off' is not allowed on a racecourse, or to work in a racing stable. From being one of the most fashionable young jockeys in the country Smirke was reduced to selling ice-creams on the sea front at Brighton. Welcome Gift was exported to India, where he showed himself to be a rogue who invariably failed to start. But it was several years before the Jockey Club relented and restored Smirke's jockey's licence at the end of the 1933 season.

The following year he was retained by Marcus Marsh to ride the Maharajah of Rajpipla's colt, Windsor Lad, in all his races. He turned up for his first gallop in a borrowed Bentley, but after Windsor Lad won the Derby and the St Leger he was once again able to afford his own. They were an unlikely collection of people to be connected with a Derby winner, since Marsh had only four horses in his stable at the time, the Maharajah of Rajpipla was having his first runner in a classic race, and Smirke had hardly ridden a winner for five years. The Maharaja was overcome by the victory and, on being congratulated by the King, he assured him that Windsor Lad was really only a very ordinary horse.

In 1935 Smirke won the St Leger on the Aga Khan's Bahram, and at the beginning of the 1936 season he was once again retained to ride the Aga Khan's horses, then trained in Newmarket by Frank Butters. Butters never trusted Smirke. He was convinced he rode in gallops only to gain information for Aly Khan to bet with, and he would often refuse to let him ride in a gallop, even if he had made a special effort to drive down from London. There was some truth in Butters's allegations, for Smirke and Aly Khan were close friends. At Goodwood in 1938, Butters ran two of the Aga Khan's fillies in the same race. Doug Smith, riding the less fancied of the two, managed to get up and beat Smirke on the other by a short head. After they had pulled up, Smirke came alongside Smith and yelled abuse at him the whole way back to the unsaddling enclosure; apparently Aly Khan had had £10,000 on Smirke's horse.

During the war, Smirke joined the army and missed five seasons of riding. At the time someone is supposed to have gone up to Butters on the gallops and said:

'Have you heard the news, Mr Butters? Charlie Smirke's been awarded the V.C. in Sicily.'

'Really? What for?'

'For stopping a German tank.'

'I am not at all surprised. When he was riding for me he would stop anything.'

Frank Butters was forced to give up his career as a trainer after he had been knocked off his bicycle by a lorry in 1949. Despite being sent by the Aga Khan to the most renowned specialists, he never fully recovered. It was Smirke who persuaded the Aga Khan to take on Marcus Marsh as his replacement, and they shared in another Derby triumph with Tulyar in 1952. Smirke used to wear a black sweater, black jodphurs, and black boots when he rode-work on Tulyar, to ensure that everyone in Newmarket knew they were watching Smirke and the Derby winner. He stayed with Marsh until 1956, when he was appointed the Aga Khan's jockey for the fourth time. However, he was unable to work with Alec Head, the new trainer, and in his final three seasons he rode only occasionally. His final Derby victory, on Hard Ridden in 1958, was one of only nineteen rides he had that year. Smirke was always more interested in winning the few big races than many small ones and he was interested in working only for those owners and trainers he personally liked. When he retired in 1959, he withdrew from the racing world completely.

For those who remembered the deferential attitude of jockeys before the First World War, the antics of Donoghue and Smirke were a matter for concern. The popular acclaim given to successful jockeys was encouraging them to hold exalted opinions of themselves and flagrantly to disobey such rules as that forbidding them to bet. The conspicuously extravagant lifestyles some of them led were not considered compatible with their responsibilities to their employers and the betting public. Men like Lord Derby and Lord Rosebery set an example of how these things could be managed. Derby sacked Tommy Weston in 1935 after employing him for eleven years, without even an explanation. At that time there were rumours circulating that Weston had either lost his nerve or was not always doing everything he could to win. Weston's rise to the top had been very swift, and he continued riding for some years; but he remained bitter, and there were always those who doubted his scrupulousness. He wrote in his autobiography: 'I learned my lesson long ago that many folks in the racing world only cultivated my acquaintance, as they do other jockeys, for all they thought they could get out of me.'[3]

Eph Smith, who rode for Lord Rosebery's trainer Jack Jarvis from 1933 to 1948, wrote in his autobiography: 'jockeys never, never retaliated when spoken to sharply or unjustly criticised. They took it and suffered in silence'.[4] The fact that he did not always follow his contemporaries' example meant that Smith got fewer rides than he might have done. He suffered from deafness; if he was ever beaten because he had stopped riding, thinking he was sure to win, he would excuse himself by saying he had not heard the other horse coming. Sir Foster Robinson was once sitting next to Smith at a dinner, long after he had retired from race riding. When someone asked Sir Foster to pass a roll, he reached over Smith and took his roll, announcing to his neighbour: 'Well, he still can't hear them coming!'

For the majority of owners and trainers, as well as for the racing public, the ideal jockey was Sir Gordon Richards. He was the most successful jockey of the era, champion twenty-six times between

1925 and 1954. Those who know him today – and it was only recently that he ceased to ride out regularly for Major Hern – maintain he is an inspiring man. His unmistakable qualities are dedication, loyalty, and honesty. He rode in about 21,000 races, winning 4,870 of them; some seasons he rode in as many as 1,000 races. Today, even with the aid of aeroplanes and night meetings, it is rare for a jockey to ride in as many. From 1932 to 1947 Richards was retained by Fred Darling, and when the latter retired, he spent the remainder of his career riding for Sir Noel Murless. He was champion in his first season as a full jockey, at the age of twenty-one.

In 1933 Richards beat Fred Archer's record of riding 248 winners in a season. The number of winners he rode each day was headline news after he had completed 100 winners by the end of June. The 200 came up on 8 September, and from then until beating the record his every movement was news. He equalled the record on the forty-eighth anniversary of the day Archer rode his last winner, and beat it on the anniversary of his death. He admitted later that the end of the season had been a nightmare, rendering him on the verge of a nervous breakdown and unable to close his eyes without visions of horses appearing. His remarkable achievement was to sustain such a level of hard work and dedication that he remained one of the very best jockeys throughout his career. He is now an honorary member of the Jockey Club, though he has withdrawn from public life since the death of his wife, Margery, to whom he had been married for over fifty years.

The combination of increased popular interest in the racing world and a more competitive demand for their services enabled jockeys to earn more, as well as enjoying more independence and prestige. The best jockeys were able to ride for their choice of the many rich newcomers, who were willing to bid against each other for their services. It took considerably longer for the training profession to move in the same direction. The main reason for this was the difficulty for someone with no family connection in the racing world to make a name for himself as a trainer. To become a jockey it is necessary to have the skills and a great deal of luck; to become a trainer, it is necessary not only to persuade owners to send you their horses, but also to inherit a stable yard or possess sufficient capital to buy one. Once a trainer has set himself up in a yard with horses, he then needs a great deal of luck to gain recognition. Between the wars most train-

The Duke of Westminster's
Ormonde, Triple Crown
winner of 1886, with
Fred Archer (*Popperfoto*)

Lord Derby's Swynford,
winner of the 1910
St Leger (*W.W. Rouch*)

(*Left*) Richard Marsh and Mrs Richard Marsh at Tattersal's Yearling Sales, Doncaster, 1924 (*Topham*)

(*Above*) *Left to right*: Richard Marsh, Lord Marcus Beresford, and King Edward VII (*W.W. Rouch*)

(*Right*) The 17th Earl of Derby (*W.W. Rouch*)

George Lambton with his family (*W.W. Rouch*)

Jack Joel (*W.W. Rouch*)

Solly Joel (*W.W. Rouch*)

Gordon Richards winning at Windsor in 1945 (*Popperfoto*)

Lord Woolavington's Captain Cuttle, trained by Fred Darling, ridden by Steve Donoghue, wins the 1922 Derby (*Popperfoto*)

Lord Glanely (centre) at
the Newmarket Yearling
Sales in 1928 with the
trainer Felix Leach and
Colonel Arthur Boyd
Rochfort (*Topham*)

Fred Darling at
Beckhampton, 1942
(*Popperfoto*)

ers inherited either their yards, their profession, or both. Of the leading trainers of the period, Alec Taylor, Fred Darling, Richard Dawson, and Marcus Marsh were all the sons of trainers. Marcus Marsh possessed almost the perfect pedigree for his job – being by Richard Marsh, Edward VII's trainer, out of Grace Darling, Fred Darling's sister.

The Newmarket training families were even more prolific, as four of James Waugh's sons, three of William Jarvis's sons, and two of Joseph Butters's sons trained there at one time or another. These three families are related by marriage, as Joseph Butters married a daughter of James Waugh's, and their eldest daughter Isabel married William Rose Jarvis, the eldest son of William Arthur Jarvis. The prominence of these traditional training families, and the fact that social prejudice still prevented many of those who had sufficient capital from setting themselves up as trainers, meant that the training profession retained a particular respect for tradition. Such men were inclined to maintain the old-fashioned deferential relationship trainers had with their owners, and a wariness of innovation.

Jack Jarvis, knighted for his services to racing in 1967, was proud of the fact that his horses were galloped three times a week, even when it had become normal for strings to be galloped twice a week. A trainer of the modern school once described Jarvis's horses as being so lean that they looked more like herrings than racehorses. Jarvis trained for the sixth Earl of Rosebery for thirty-nine years and, despite both having a reputation for being difficult men, they became close friends. Throughout their long partnership Lord Rosebery addressed his letters to 'Jarvis' and signed them simply 'R.'

Coming from an old racing family did not necessarily imply either a disinclination to innovate or a deferential attitude, for Fred Darling cannot be said to have displayed either characteristic. As well as being the outstanding trainer of his time, he was an individual. He trained for some years before taking over his father's Beckhampton stables in 1913. He had won the Cesarewitch for Lady de Bathe, the former actress Lillie Langtry, and spent some time training in Germany, where he was married. His wife returned to Germany in 1914, and although he never saw her again he was never heard to say a word against her, and her picture always remained on the wall at Beckhampton. Darling's training methods were a complete departure from the traditional; he was the first man to produce his horses blooming in their coat and carrying some condition, at the same time as being fully fit. Before his enormous success, any horse appearing in the paddock in such a condition would have been dismissed as being obviously in need of a race before reaching its peak. The 'Beckhampton bloom' is said by some to have been the result of using arsenic tonics. Jeremy Tree, who knew Darling at the end of his life, holds this to be an absurd idea; for although Darling was always ready to try any new tonic on the market, he never used any particular drug consistently enough for it to have been the cause of the superb condition of his horses.

Darling went to any lengths to know his horses as individuals and then to persuade them to do their best on the day that mattered. He employed Joe Childs to ride Coronach, even though he disliked him as a man, then persuaded him to lead all the way in the Derby – a style of riding Childs found offensive. Childs is said to have stormed into the weighing room afterwards, hurled his saddle on the table, and yelled: 'What a bloody way to ride a horse!'

Darling made his plans as to where his horses were going to run three weeks in advance; nothing bar sickness would alter them. He had not the slightest interest in what any other stable was running. Most trainers spend time looking at the entries for each race in order to find the easiest winning opportunities for their charges. The plans for his two-year-olds would be decided at the beginning of the season, when they were divided up into Ascot two-year-olds, Goodwood two-year-olds, and the rest, in whom he had no interest. If an owner interfered, suggesting he might like his horse to run at Royal Ascot, he would be told in that case he had better send it to someone else. Darling would not accept the slightest breach of discipline from either man or horse. Nevertheless, those who worked with him and knew him well speak of him with affection.

Marcus Marsh, who was his assistant before falling out over the stable's arrangements for betting, adored him. He tells how Darling used to take great care to discourage owners from coming to see their horses. If an owner ventured to go out with the string on a hack, Darling would arrange with Marsh to jump a railing unexpectedly on the way back to the yard, in the hope that the owner's hack would follow and catch its rider unawares: many owners ended their visits to Beckhampton deposited on the ground. Occasionally

Marsh and Darling would go to London together for the evening, leaving a night-club at three-thirty in the morning to arrive back at Beckhampton in time for a bath, before supervising the first lot. Darling was also keen on aeroplanes. He used to persuade Marcus Wickham Boynton to join him on day trips to Newmarket, having hired a plane for the day from Croydon airfield.

People speak with awe of some of the idiosyncrasies of Darling's training and his dedication. He always worked his two-year-olds so that they finished going downhill, in order to give them confidence. Sir Gordon Richards, his stable jockey for sixteen seasons, is supposed to have said that in his opinion Cecil Boyd Rochfort would never train the winner of the Derby; for his 'guvnor' would start his classic horses in February, in order to have them in work by April – at which time Boyd Rochfort would still be on holiday. He was wrong, as Boyd Rochfort trained Parthia to win the 1959 Derby.

Although not a man who found it easy to show emotion, when Darling was excited about a horse he would speak of it in the first person. He rang up Marcus Marsh before the 1935 Coronation Cup, in which his horse Easton was due to take on Marsh's Derby winner Windsor Lad, to say: 'I think you ought to know that I have just given Montrose twenty-one pounds and made a hack of him.'[5] His confidence was misplaced, as Windsor Lad won the race easily.

Fred Darling was champion trainer on six occasions, training the winners of nineteen classic races, including seven Derby winners. He died three days after listening to the commentary on Pinza's Derby. He had bred Pinza himself; the horse was trained by Norman Bertie, who had been his travelling head lad, and ridden by Gordon Richards. Apparently Darling showed no surprise or elation, but he told those who congratulated him that he had always known Pinza would win. Marcus Marsh said that Darling had never been afraid of dying, only of dying before Pinza's Derby.

Today, it would be impossible to train in the manner of Fred Darling – not least because the rise in the wages of stable staff has meant that such a labour-intensive operation is too expensive, even for the richest of Arabs. It is also doubtful if any of today's top trainers could afford to be so inconsiderate to their owners, since, with the exception of Vincent O'Brien, they all compete for the custom of much the same people. Darling's record as a trainer was such that, whatever his personal reputation, there were always people willing to send him their horses. There is no stable today run under such a militaristic code of discipline: not only did Darling's lads have to follow a severe routine, but they were expected to be as immaculate in appearance as their charges, riding out in tweed caps and jackets with polished boots and leggings.

In less affluent yards, stable lads in general, and apprentices in particular, were often exploited. Apprentice jockeys were paid little, and any money they earned from riding went into their master's pocket; the idea was that it would be returned to them at the end of their apprenticeship, when they were old enough to use it responsibly. Doug Smith, who was to become champion jockey, was apprenticed to Major Sneyd. He was successful as a boy, riding his first winner when he was fifteen; not long afterwards he rode his first treble, one Saturday at Ripon. To ensure that he did not acquire an 'exalted opinion of himself', Sneyd made him spend the following day weeding his drive. Smith was given a seven-pound Dundee cake by Lyons, after his treble had been judged the best sporting achievement of the week. Sneyd appropriated the cake and told him a few days later: 'You write and thank them. It was a good cake, you know.'[6]

When writing on the art of training, H.S. – known as 'Atty' – Persse defended his treatment of his lads by comparing his stable to a public school:

> To enter a calling which offers kindred rewards to those dangled before the jockey, the sons of gentlemen have to study long years, for no pay, and their fathers have to bear heavy expenses. The treatment of boys in stables is no harder than that of the average public school boy in his school, usually not so hard; and so he need not complain of the rigours of his lot.[7]

Public-school boys, however, were occasionally allowed out on holiday, and this is also an unfair comparison because the number of apprentices who managed to establish themselves as jockeys was very small. The lot of boys in stables was made considerably harder by the need for complete secrecy about the relative merits and well-being of the stable's inmates.

Before the capital value of the racehorse increased to a level at which it was possible to pay for a horse's career by selling it as a potential broodmare, stallion, or hurdler, most owners and trainers looked to betting to cover their costs. This only partly explains the prodigious scale of gambling between the wars and the lengths to which bookmakers and gamblers went to find out what happened on private gallops. The most famous professional gambler of the period was Charles Hannam, who was reputed to have an annual turnover of £2 million; he was ruined when Domaka failed to win the 1938 Cambridgeshire.

There were a number of professional gallop watchers, or touts as they were commonly called, who would discreetly observe gallops and then sell their information – either to bookmakers, who could then reduce the odds they were offering on a horse that had worked particularly well, or to gamblers, who could back the same horse. Being a Newmarket tout was never a job for the lazy, as it involved being on the Heath six days a week and being able to recognize every horse in the town by sight – a matter of thousands rather than hundreds. Colonel Tom Nickals, who was the *Sporting Life*'s Newmarket correspondent, used to win money on the ability of his tout, 'Chippy' Jackson, to remember a horse. He was once asked to name a particular horse who was trained in the West Country and just staying in Newmarket for a race; Jackson named it correctly, because he had once seen it run at Bath.

It was considered perfectly fair to impede touts, or even to prevent them physically from carrying out their business, although the more astute trainers were content to outwit them. Victor Gilpin used to fool them by placing weights in the saddle-cloths of his horses before they galloped. He was once training a filly of Lord Wavertree's called Midge; he made no secret of considering her to be much improved, so that when he galloped her a week before her intended race, in the north of England, a fair crowd turned up to watch her performance. She finished last of the four horses in the gallop and a disappointed Gilpin explained to those watching that he must have been mistaken. The truth, as he told his assistant John Hislop, was that Midge had been carrying considerable extra weight and on her form in the gallop was a certainty for the race. Midge was sent up to the North in the sole charge of a particularly simple lad called Ernest Appleby, whom no one would have expected to be entrusted with a horse that was sure to win. On the day of the race Hislop was taken out on a rough shoot, far away from any bookmakers. Much to the surprise of the Newmarket touts, Midge won her race easily.

This obsession with secrecy led to all journalists, stable lads, and even other trainers being treated with the utmost suspicion. Tom Nickals remembers staying on the gallops one day after the second lot, in order to watch Tehran, then a four-year-old and a leading contender for the Ascot Gold Cup, do some work. After watching the gallop he went up to his trainer, Frank Butters, and asked where he was planning to run the horse, only to be told: 'The future engagements of Tehran are the sole concern of myself and His Highness the Aga Khan.'

One of the more successful gambling trainers was 'Atty' Persse. He was not interested in winning the major races, as the joy of training was for him to find out how good his horses were at home and then to have £1,000 on them on their first appearance. Thus it was essential for Persse that stable secrets remained secret. He considered any stable lad seen with new clothes a criminal; for how could they afford them on what he was paying, other than by selling stable information? Persse gave his lads more responsibility than Frank Hartigan did; he was so convinced of the potential criminality of his employees that his yearling boxes had only numbers on them: even the lad looking after a particular horse would not know its name until it had run.

Trainers generally held themselves aloof from each other, not only because they had no wish to discuss their horses with competitors (few successful trainers have time for outside interests), but because of the usual animosity and jealousy between members of the same profession. Further friction was added by the status awarded to those trainers who who were considered to be 'gentlemen'. John Hislop remembers that, when he was thinking about becoming a trainer, he was warned he had better become a member of Newmarket first, as he was certain to be refused if he applied afterwards. The only trainers allowed in the members' enclosure at Newmarket were those like Cecil Boyd Rochfort, George Lambton, and Victor Gilpin whose breeding was held to be of the same standard as their ability to train. Similar snobbery was prevalent in the Newmarket social clubs, with the Subscription Rooms being considered smarter than the Craven Club; both establishments were forced to close down, as trainers chose to do their drinking elsewhere.

Cecil Boyd Rochfort, who was created K.C.V.O. in 1968, joined 'Atty' Persse as a pupil-trainer on leaving Eton in 1906. He worked as racing manager to both Sir Ernest Cassel and the American millionaire Marshall Field, before setting up as a trainer at Freemason Lodge in Newmarket in 1923; he remained there until his retirement in 1968. The main advantage for a man from a background like Boyd Rochfort's was that many of his friends and relations could afford to send him horses to train. Boyd Rochfort was particularly successful with the horses of some of the wealthy Americans he had met through Marshall Field. The advantage he had, over someone from a similar background who starts training today, was that it was then possible both to train for your friends and to train the best racehorses. The cost of the best racehorses today means that the two are unlikely to coincide. Considering the length of his career, it is not surprising that by the end of it Sir Cecil Boyd Rochfort had acquired a reputation as a traditionalist. In the 1960s he maintained the discipline and style common to the stables of Newmarket in the 1930s. Harry Carr, his stable jockey for seventeen seasons, wrote that to arrive for a gallop of Boyd Rochfort's without a cap on would have been as humiliating as arriving naked. When he retired, Boyd Rochfort handed over his string to his stepson Henry Cecil.

Boyd Rochfort had a famous feud with Sir Jack Jarvis. The only occasion they were seen to converse was when starting stalls were first demonstrated at Newmarket. After the horses had jumped out, without doing themselves any obvious injury, Boyd Rochfort turned to Jarvis and exclaimed: 'Damn, they work!' In his younger days he was something of a gambler, a habit he never completely lost, although like Fred Darling at the end of his career he liked to pretend that he had. The success he had before the Second World War – he was champion trainer in 1937 and 1938 – must have encouraged others from similar backgrounds to become trainers and thus to help make training a more competitive profession, no longer confined to the members of a few families.

Before looking at the state of British horse-racing after the Second World War, it is worth considering in some detail the character and racing career of the third Aga Khan. The Aga Khan was a catalyst for change: he was an outsider, and thus no respecter of racing's conventions and less fearful of the approbation of the racing establishment than most of the other leading owners of the time. But he was also a man with considerable stature outside the racing world, and one of the few brilliant men to have spent time studying horse-racing and breeding. The planning and management of his racing operation are of particular contemporary interest as he was the first man to attempt to race and breed thoroughbreds on the scale now emulated by the Maktoum family of Dubai and Prince Khaled Abdulla.

5

The Aga Khan

His Highness Aga Sultan Sir Mohammed Shah, the third Aga Khan, was the first man to race on a large scale and to be internationally based. At the peak of his operations he owned five studs in Ireland, another four in France, and over 100 broodmares. In the years between 1922 and 1952, when he moved his horses to France, the Aga Khan was the leading owner in Britain on thirteen occasions and the leading breeder eight times. He is the only owner to have won the Derby five times, and he and his son Aly Khan won a further fifteen classic races in England, as well as at least ten French and Irish classics.

He raced horses in India from his youth, but waited until after the First World War, when he could afford to race on a scale that suited him, before starting to buy horses in Europe. Although he was an expert on breeding he took on George Lambton to select yearlings on their conformation. He asked Lambton to train for him as well, but Lambton remained loyal to Lord Derby. On the recommendation of Colonel Hall Walker, with whom he had been friendly since the turn of the century, he took on Lieutenant-Colonel Vuillier as his breeding expert. After leaving the French Air Force, Colonel Vuillier spent many years formulating what he called 'the dosage system' of inheritance of the thoroughbred.[1] This system, since elaborated upon by Dr Franco Varola, is now widely dismissed in the trade as an eccentric irrelevance, although to some extent the Aga Khan's breeding operation was based upon it.

Many traditionalists viewed the Aga Khan's successes with distaste because of his business-like approach. His son, Aly Khan, once said: 'Father and I are just a couple of horse traders. Some people are in this business for fun; we're in it for profit.'[2] The only men to have invested in bloodstock since on a similar scale – Marcel Boussac, Robert Sangster, the Maktoum family of Dubai, and Prince Khaled Abdulla – have also found it hard to please everyone. If a man spends enormous sums of money on horses he is likely to be called a fool, but if he attempts to run a bloodstock empire on lines similar to a business he will be accused of demeaning the sport of horse-racing.

The Aga Khan did not make money out of horse-racing, however; nor did he intend to. In his day, the most promising young stallions were worth only £45,000 – the figure for which he sold Blenheim a few weeks after his son Mahmoud had won the Derby. Yet he estimated his racing and breeding establishments cost £250,000 a year to run. He said that he looked upon his racing as 'a source of pleasure not only to ourselves but for thousands, indeed for millions, who follow our colours on the turf'.[3]

The third Aga Khan was born in 1877. On his father's death in 1885 he became the Imam of the Ismailis, being considered by them to be forty-eighth in direct male descent from the Prophet Mohammed, to whose line they had declared allegiance until the Prophet's son-in-law, Ali, should return to the earth and judge the world. No one seems to know exactly how many Ismailis there are, but the figure is probably millions. In 1885, they were spread throughout India, Persia, Burma, South-east Asia, East Africa, and Egypt, although today there are also many in Europe. The Aga Khan derived his huge wealth from the tribute he received from his followers. He saw his role as more than that of a spiritual leader. He always tried to guide the Ismailis politically and socially, as well as making decisions in the intellectual Koranic debates. When he first entered political life his liberalism led him to be thought of as a 'radical' by the British administration in India. By the end of his life, his assumption that the British would always have a role to play in the government of India, and that Moslem countries should aspire to emulate what he considered to be the social and technological advances of the Western world, detached him from radical Moslem and Indian politicians.

Many of the Westerners he came into contact with found it hard to reconcile the chubby lover of beautiful women and horses – the habitué of casinos, night-clubs and golf courses – with their idea of God's representative on earth; they considered the deference shown to him by his followers ridiculous. However, the ambiguity of his position never tormented the Aga Khan. Most of the Westerners who knew him saw him as a man worthy of respect. One of his trainers, Marcus Marsh, wrote that although the idea of man being a god was foreign to him, he never met anyone more suited to the role.

In the years leading up to the First World War, the Aga Khan became convinced of the physical and mental benefits of taking part in sport, in his own case golf. He was sure the reason why he was always on the large side was that he had spent his youth studying to the exclusion of any exercise; a more likely explanation was his passion for good food. There are numerous legends about his consumption. He once invited his jockey, Charlie Smirke, to come and see him in the Ritz about mid-morning. When Smirke arrived, he told him he had ordered them both some crab. Smirke was forced to decline the offer, as he was having trouble with his weight, and to watch the Aga Khan eat two whole crabs with obvious delight. He once arrived to stay with Marcus Marsh at Newmarket, announcing that Marsh need not worry about food as he was on a diet. Marsh was not surprised to see that, despite their master's diet, his servants arrived with packing cases full of fruit and wild delicacies. He was surprised when he gave the Aga Khan a melon to cut up for the party at dinner, to see him slice the top off and eat it like an egg!

When war was declared with Germany in 1914, the Aga Khan ordered all Ismailis to do everything possible to support their King Emperor. In the years between the wars, he saw himself as a roving ambassador for Britain's colonial subjects, speaking particularly on behalf of the Moslems. It was a role he considered himself well qualified for, with his background, and his friendship with King George V and many of the leading British politicians of the day. His presence at the London Round Table Conference on the future of India provoked criticism from his Indian political opponents. Nehru wrote: 'It was fitting that in this assembly of vested interests, imperialist, feudal, financial, industrial, religious, communal, the leadership of the British Indian delegation should fall to the Aga Khan, who in his own person happened to combine all these interests to some degree.'[4]

By the 1930s, however, what influence he had had on Indian politics was declining, although he represented India at the Disarmament Conference in Geneva in 1932. He was sitting in the hall of the

League of Nations when his colt Bahram completed his Triple Crown by winning the 1935 St Leger. It was with great pride that he told the press: 'I doubt if any other member of the assembly has ever been called away to hear that his horse has won the St Leger.'

There were many who refused to talk to the Aga Khan after the war because they felt that, for a time at least, he had supported Hitler. Such suppositions were partly the result of his term as President of the League of Nations when, like many western conservatives, he found much to admire in Hitler's Germany. He wrote to *The Times* to say that he doubted Hitler meant what he said in *Mein Kampf* and that he saw no reason to suspect that Hitler did not intend to respect existing national boundaries. In October 1937, he visited Germany, at Hitler's invitation. Hitler showed an interest in the Aga's racing and asked him, over tea at Berchtesgaden, how much a good stallion was worth. On being told that the figure was about £30,000, Hitler asked if he would exchange thirty cars for one stallion. The Aga Khan is supposed to have replied: 'What would I do with them? I don't want to open a motor shop in Piccadilly.'

When war was declared, the Aga Khan hastily retired from the South of France, to the safety of Switzerland. Afterwards he wrote that he never set foot outside Switzerland for the duration of the war. This was not true, for in 1942 he made a brief visit to the South of France. It was reported in England that he had been seen in Paris and Berlin, and a German agent in Geneva wrote a letter to the German Foreign Office, claiming that the Aga Khan and the Khedive of Egypt had expressed a wish to join Hitler for a bottle of champagne on his first night in Windsor Castle; such claims have never been substantiated.

If the Aga Khan for a time doubted the allies' ability to succeed, he was certainly not alone; nor would he have been alone amongst his countrymen if he had considered a German victory to be desirable. Such a desire would, however, have been contrary to all his expressed hopes for India and a negation of his political life. It has been suggested that he became disillusioned with Britain after 1932 and that he was hurt by the refusal of the British to take seriously his request for a sovereign Ismaili State in northern India. His son, Aly Khan, dismissed such insinuations as 'nonsensical', adding, 'My father fought all his life for Britain.' Throughout the war all the stakes won by his horses were handed to the Indian Army Fund.

The Aga Khan came in for considerable criticism when he sold his first Derby winner, Blenheim, to the United States in 1936. The sale was understandable, as he had not bred Blenheim, but his son Mahmoud, who came from the best family in the Aga Khan's stud, had just won the Derby and looked to be a suitable replacement. In 1940 he sold both Mahmoud and Bahram to the United States, as well as selling most of his yearlings without reserve, decisions that may have been the result of a conviction that the allies were unlikely to win the war and that it was likely to last many years. Some have claimed he offered both stallions to the National Stud but got no response, or that he offered all his bloodstock for sale for £1 million, without finding a buyer. If the former was the case, then it would not be the only time the National Stud lost a great stallion through incompetence. Charles Englehard had tentatively arranged with the Jockey Club for Nijinsky to stand at the National Stud before the matter was taken out of their hands. The man who took over negotiations took so long to draw up an agreement that by the time he had finished, Nijinsky was in Kentucky, where he has stayed ever since.

In 1943, the word reached the Khan studs in Ireland that they were to stop selling yearlings. This was taken to mean he considered the war to be reaching a conclusion. In 1945 he sold a half-share in all his bloodstock to his son Aly, and ceased to play much of a role in public life.

Aly Khan saw little of his father when he was young. The Aga Khan was not impressed by English public schools, so he sent his son to a private tutorial near Oxford. Here he became friends with Michael Beary and under his tutelage became a good amateur jockey, winning over 100 races. What he enjoyed most about racing, however, was buying and selling horses at a profit.

His skill at judging horses could annoy his father, as for example the time when he sold Foxglove II to his great friend, the Hon. Peter Beatty, the day before he won the Gold Vase at Royal Ascot. He registered his own colours, green with a red sash: the Ismaili colours that had been unavailable when his father registered his green and chocolate hoops, and chocolate cap. He often deputized for his father on the racecourse and, despite his considerable reputation as a 'womanizer', once on the racecourse he generally immersed himself in racing talk with racing men.

The Aga Khan and his son always had their differences. Their ideas on racing at times conflicted, particularly during the last five years of the Aga Khan's life, when for the first time in thirty years their stables went through a lean patch; they had only one classic winner, Rose Royale, who won the One Thousand Guineas in 1957, the year of the Aga Khan's death. He stated in his will that he desired to be buried near the Nile, in the hope that, like the Pharaohs before him, his body would be preserved for some time. His widow, the Begum, still lives nearby, on an island in the Nile.

Aly Khan outlived his father by only three years, dying in a car crash in Paris in 1960. In 1959 he enjoyed a last triumphant racing season, becoming the first owner to win over £100,000 in prize money in England, largely due to his superlative filly Petite Étoile. That season she was the unbeaten winner of six races: the Free Handicap, the One Thousand Guineas, the Oaks, the Sussex Stakes, the Yorkshire Oaks, and the Champion Stakes.

It would be easy to look at the facts of Aly Khan's life and conclude that he left unfulfilled considerably more than he actually achieved. His inherent restlessness with people and places, his almost compulsive gambling, and the fact he was able to say the war years were some of the happiest of his life, suggests something of a sad character, never completely at ease with the roles he was expected to play.

Yet he is remembered by his contemporaries with something approaching awe and, of course, his lifestyle and his success with women and horses was admired and envied by many. The mention of his name to those like Frank Vogel and Alec Head, who knew him well, is likely to produce an unexpected show of emotion.

Frank Vogel describes him as simply the most charming man that ever lived; he was loyal and kind to his friends, not in the least arrogant or ostentatious with his money. If he went out to dinner he would tip everyone from the doorman to the waiter, and if Frank took him out to dinner he would take the cheque when he was not looking. When they were in Deauville, where they each had villas, they would ride on the beach together before breakfast and play bridge twice a week, for small sums because Aly loved to play. Every morning Frank would go to Aly and say he refused to let Aly pay for him, and every morning Aly would tell him, 'Don't worry Frank, you can start paying tomorrow.' According to Frank, Aly was determined to live life to the full and he succeeded completely.

If any Khan is a sad character he says, it is Aly's son Karim, the present Aga Khan.

The Aga Khan had started buying racehorses in Europe in 1921. From the beginning his objectives were grand and long term. George Lambton's reputation as a judge of horses was surpassing, and Richard Dawson, whom Lambton suggested as a suitable trainer, was already well established as he had trained Fifinella to win the Derby and the Oaks in 1916. These two men spent £275,000 at yearling sales on the Aga Khan's behalf between 1921 and 1929. They were acting under instructions to buy the best fillies on the market, whatever the price (some of the prices they paid were thought to be ridiculously high), with a view to gathering together the finest collection of broodmares in Europe.

They also bought a few colts, but the emphasis was on fillies. This was because it was rare for a potential classic colt to be sent to the sales, and anyway the Aga Khan was more interested in breeding classic winners than in buying them. As regards his breeding operation, the Aga Khan realized that it was not essential to own the best stallions, as he could afford to buy shares in, or nominations to, any stallion he desired. This is the way most large breeding operations are planned today, with nearly all stallions being syndicated and standing at specialist stud farms. Yet the two other major breeders of the time, Lord Derby and Marcel Boussac, both maintained the traditional approach, retaining their best colts and then using them to cover their best mares. Colonel Vuillier, who immediately took control of the breeding operation, always said that whereas most people looked to the stallion to provide excellence in a mating, he was more interested in the mare.

The Aga Khan also recognized that even a man of his wealth could not afford to run such a large operation without receiving a return, other than any prize money his horses might win. He was always prepared to sell any colt if he was offered enough for it, and he sold all five of his Derby winners, as well as the outstanding stallions Nasrullah and Alibhai. He continually bought and sold broodmares, and offered a proportion of his yearlings for sale every year. For a breeding operation of any size to maintain the highest level of success, it must always be prepared to try new blood. The Aga Khan was ready to sell mares from his most renowned families if he thought their prepotency was on the wane; until the end of his life he avoided the mistake of making allowances for the failings of his own stallions and continuing to use them when there were other more suitable stallions available.

He intended to run his racing empire on business-like lines. He employed only the best men, he bought only the best horses, and he was willing to be ruthless with both men and horses, avoiding sentimentality when making every decision. At the beginning the delegation of responsibility was clear, and he came as close as possible to having a comprehensive plan for each category – buying, racing, and breeding – as well as an overall strategy. His objective was to breed a large number of top class racehorses every season, and thus to dominate British racing for his lifetime.

Success came immediately. The first batch of yearlings the Aga Khan bought included Cos, who was champion two-year-old filly in 1922 and later produced three top class winners. The following year Richard Dawson bought him Friar's Daughter for only 250 guineas. She won only one small race, but among her eleven winning offspring were Dastur, who was placed in three classic races, and the Triple Crown winner Bahram. The same year Lambton bought him the Two Thousand Guineas winner Diophon, Salmon Trout, who won the St Leger, and the famous filly Mumtaz Mahal. This last was named after the favourite wife of the Shah Jahan, who built for her the Taj Mahal mausoleum.

The grey daughter of The Tetrarch became known as 'Mumty' or 'The Flying Filly', after she had won her first five races very easily indeed, winning at Royal Ascot by ten lengths. She narrowly lost the last race of her two-year-old career, failing to stay on heavy ground, and as a three-year-old she was beaten in her three races over a mile. Reverting to sprinting, she won her last two races brilliantly. Her own offspring were disappointing on the racecourse, but her daughters and their descendants bred the Derby winner Mahmoud, the Two Thousand Guineas winner Abernant, Petite Étoile, the Prix de l'Arc de Triomphe winner Migoli, and the great stallion Nasrullah. In 1924, the third season in which his horses took part, the Aga Khan was the leading owner in Britain.

For the next thirty years he had one or two runners in every major race. When Firdaussi won the St Leger in 1932, the Aga Khan also owned the horses that finished second, fourth, and fifth. Seven of his horses were placed in the Derby, in addition to the five who were successful. George Lambton made a rare mistake when he advised him not to buy Papyrus as a yearling, but he atoned by purchasing the Aga Khan's first Derby winner, Blenheim, for 4,100 guineas. Among the many broodmares the Aga Khan bought to introduce new blood to his stud were Neocracy, who bred nine winners including the Derby winner Tulyar and the Prix de l'Arc de Triomphe winner Saint Crespin III, and Uganda. He had to buy a stud in France and all the bloodstock of Ed Kaun to obtain Uganda, but she was worth it, for she bred two classic winners and the dam of Palestine, who won the Two Thousand Guineas. Among the proven racehorses he bought were My Love, who won the Derby and the Grand Prix de Paris in the month following his purchase, and Nuccio, who was successful in the Prix de l'Arc de Triomphe, wearing the Aga Khan's chocolate and green colours.

The bloodstock market was less competitive in the Aga Khan's time than it is today. If he was determined to buy a horse, there were few men wealthy enough to outbid him. At that time the best racehorses were bought and sold in England, with only a few exceptions, sparing him and his advisers the necessity of following the bloodstock circus to Ireland, the United States, Canada, and Australia. Yet the results the Aga Khan achieved were largely due to meticulous planning. As long as his original advisers were alive and he abided by the rules he had set himself, ignoring sentimental arguments and being prepared to innovate and change, he was able to win Europe's top races regularly.

By the 1950s, however, it was plain that the standard of the Aga Khan's horses was declining. Vuillier and Lambton had not been replaced by men of a similar calibre, and Aly Khan was not as thorough an administrator as his father. He persisted in buying staying blood when the emphasis had shifted towards speed, and he used his own stallions Tehran and Migoli even when they failed to realize his expectations. The broodmares the Aga Khan and Aly Khan bought at this time did not found dynasties in the way Uganda and Mumtaz Mahal had done; Petite Étoile did not produce a single winner. The Khan studs went through a quiet period of about twenty years, when their major winners were few and far between. It may have been that the family's luck had run out, but as careful planning played a large role during the years of success, so the lack of it contributed to the decline.

The Aga Khan and Aly Khan added a great deal of colour to the racing world; that such glamorous and well-known men chose to spend so much time on British racecourses stimulated popular interest. They moved their horses to France in 1952 – not on a whim, nor because the prize money was markedly higher, but because it was clear that France was the place to keep racehorses, particularly for men with their tastes.

6

The French Era

The first great French racehorse was Gladiateur, who was hailed as the 'avenger of Waterloo' when he won the 1865 Derby. According to French reports, he won despite a plot to seize his jockey, with the intention of bleeding him so he would be too weak to ride a proper race. After Epsom, Gladiateur was sent to France, where he won the Grand Prix de Paris in front of 150,000 excited and patriotic spectators. His other notable victories included the Two Thousand Guineas, the St Leger, the Ascot Gold Cup, and four other races in Paris. At the main entrance of Longchamp racecourse there is a statue of a magnificent and beautiful thoroughbred that purports to depict Count de Lagrange's Gladiateur; in fact Gladiateur was overgrown and bony, and had bad forelegs, as a result of being trodden on as a foal.

It was a long time before the supremacy of the British thoroughbred was again challenged by a horse from across the Channel. Durbar II, who won the 1914 Derby, was trained in France, but he was an American horse; his owner had brought his horses to Europe only after the passing of the anti-betting bill in New York. There was no racing at all in France during the First World War. Although some breeders attempted to test their own horses in private gallops, such a disruption meant that the top French races were of a poor standard in the years afterwards, and many of them were won by English horses. The first Prix de l'Arc de Triomphe was won by Comrade, who was trained by P. P. Gilpin at Newmarket, although he was owned by a Frenchman, Evremond de St Alary.

The most brilliant French horse to race in England between the wars was Épinard – known as 'Le Cheval Volant'. He was owned and bred by Pierre Wertheimer, who was later to win the Derby with Lavandin. As a two-year-old in 1922 he won six of his seven races; he was never entered in the classics, so, after he had won four races in Paris the following spring it was decided to run him at Goodwood in the Steward's Cup, where his connections hoped he might start at a good price. He was backed from twelve to one, to seven to two, and won in a canter, despite carrying a record weight. He was then backed for the Cambridgeshire as if he were already past the post, even though he was set to carry nine stone and two pounds; he was beaten only a neck, after wandering all over the course. The filly who beat him, Verdict, was receiving one stone and four pounds: she went on to win one of the top weight-for-age races, the Coronation Cup, the following year. Épinard was sent to race in the United States, but by that time he was past his best.

The history of French racing from 1928 to 1956 is in effect the history of Marcel Boussac and his horses. Marcel Boussac raced the winners of twelve Prix du Jockey Club, six Prix de l'Arc de Triomphe, five Prix de Diane, one English Derby, one English Oaks, two Ascot Gold Cups, seven of its French equivalent the Prix du Cadran, two St Legers, assorted Guineas, as well as endless top two-year-old races.[1] His greatest season was in 1950, when his stable won six classic races: in France, the 'Jockey Club' with Scratch, and the One Thousand Guineas with Corejada; in England, the Derby with Galcador, the Oaks with Asmena, and the St Leger with Scratch; and in Ireland, the Oaks, again with Corejada. In the same year, six of the nine best two-year-olds to have raced in France were owned and bred by Boussac, and he believed that his best two-year-olds were yet to run. He was the leading owner and breeder in England in 1950 and 1951. In 1950 his trainer, Charles Semblat, was the leading trainer in England without setting foot in the country. In 1956 he was the leading owner in France for the nineteenth time.

Boussac derived his wealth from textiles. By 1918 he had succeeded in building up a considerable business empire in France and so turned his attention to racing, with every intention of being as successful in that field. He wanted to prove that a man like himself, with a lot of money to spend but with no background in racing, could set up a pre-eminent breeding operation. Unlike many rich men with similar ideas, he bought all his horses himself and arranged the matings of his mares entirely on his own; the only specialists he employed for any length of time were the jockeys Charlie Elliott and Rae Johnstone. He would often supervise his horses' training. Rae Johnstone was once asked to ride a horse of his, which was strongly fancied for the Epsom Derby, in his last piece of work before the race. Johnstone was met by Boussac, who told him to work the colt flat out for a mile. Johnstone thought it would be stupid to do this so close to the race, so he came a mile at half speed. When he was pulling up, Boussac appeared in something of a frenzy and told him that he had disobeyed his instructions; he ordered him to get off the horse immediately. A stable lad was then put up and the horse made to do a mile at full speed: he was not even placed in the Derby.

In 1919 Boussac bought his first stud, the Harras de Jardy in Saint Cloud. Its previous owner, Edmond Blanc, answered those who said it would be impossible to breed good horses so close to Paris by asserting that he could breed the winner of the Grand Prix in the Place de la Concorde provided he could feed him what he wanted to. When Charlie Elliott, who had been English champion jockey at the age of twenty, left England fearful of rumours that the stewards were out to get him, as a result of his prodigious betting, Boussac was quick to take him on as stable jockey. Elliott rode Tourbillon, his 'Jockey Club' winner, in 1931.

The success of the Boussac studs was largely due to his owning four of the best stallions in the world at that time: Asterus, Tourbillon, Pharis, and Djebel. Pharis, who had small horns, was undefeated. He was due to run in the 1939 St Leger, against Lord Rosebery's brilliant Derby winner Blue Peter, but their meeting was cancelled upon the declaration of war; this cancellation led to the remark that only an uncivilized nation like the Germans could declare war before a great race like the St Leger. In fact, Pharis had broken down before 3 September, so the match would not have taken place anyway. Djebel won the 1940 Two Thousand Guineas and would almost certainly have won the Derby as well, if the fall of France had not prevented him from taking part.

Racing in France continued throughout the Second World War, although some of the leading figures, like Leon Volterra and Rae Johnstone, were interned. When it was possible to send runners across the Channel again, Boussac sent one of his slower horses to run against the English champion Court Martial; he discovered what he wanted: Court Martial managed only to beat him by a short head. From 1947 until 1960 there was only one season in which a French-trained runner did not win an English classic. The French horses sent to race in England were frequently nowhere near the best of their age group in France. When Galcador won the Derby in 1950, Boussac considered he had three even better colts. A list of the big races Boussac won in Britain between 1947 and 1956 would be very long; he won them all at some time, and most of them quite frequently.

The problem for Boussac was that, as most of his horses were by one of his four great stallions, when they died he either had to replace them with new blood or to intensify his already marked experiments with inbreeding. His attempts to buy American stallions were a failure and, although his inbreeding worked for a time, the produce became increasingly fragile and highly strung. He had always been hard on his horses, and many of the most promising had broken down. Pharis died in 1957, and Djebel in 1958. Without them he had to wait a long time for his next classic winner, for from 1956 until his death in 1980 Marcel Boussac raced only two classic winners. Yet the Aga Khan is thought to have paid between $8 and $9 million for what remained of his bloodstock.

By the end of the 1970s there were rumours that all was not well with the Boussac textile industry. In 1978 it was declared insolvent, and Boussac himself became bankrupt, after pouring his personal fortune into the firm. His last good colt, the 'Jockey Club' winner Acamas, had already been sold when he ran in the 1978 King George VI and Queen Elizabeth II Stakes; out of sentiment for a broken man he was allowed to run in the famous orange with a grey cap. Marcel Boussac died in 1980 at the age of ninety-one; even those who had no cause to like him were sorry and surprised that a man who had shown himself to be so astute should have contrived to end his life in such a pitiful financial position. There were many who had no liking for him; he was considered arrogant and was never elected to the French Jockey Club (now no more than an exclusive social club). He was, however, president of the Société d'Encouragement des Races de Chevaux en France from 1960 until his resignation in 1974.

Leon Volterra was another French owner who had a large influence on English racing. Born into a humble background, he made his fortune in the theatre, becoming Paris's leading impresario. The

Nuit de Longchamp in July 1935, when race-goers were invited to attend an evening meeting in evening dress, was one of his more flamboyant ideas. He had the misfortune of breeding and selling two Derby winners, Bois Roussel and My Love, though he still owned a half-share in My Love when he won the Derby in the colours of the Aga Khan.

Volterra's great ambition was to win the Derby with a horse that carried his own colours. The 1949 Derby was clearly to be his last chance, for he was very ill indeed by this time; his health had been ruined by his internment during the war. His colt Amour Drake started third favourite and after a close race went past the post looked together with Nimbus and Swallow Tail. This was the first year that the result of the Derby was determined by a photo finish, and in those days it took a long time for the result to be known. In an awful state, Volterra waited in bed to hear the result on a wireless; eventually his wife came in and told him Johnstone had managed to force Amour Drake ahead on the line. Volterra lapsed into unconsciousness and died the same night. In fact, Nimbus had held on to win by a head from Amour Drake, an unlucky loser, who had to be switched to the rails when Nimbus and Swallow Tail drifted out in front of him.

His widow, Mme 'Suzie' Volterra, took over her husband's stud and gained a proper Derby success with Phil Drake in 1955.

In the 1930s and 1940s the two best jockeys riding in Paris were Charlie Elliott and Rae Johnstone. Johnstone was born in New South Wales and became champion jockey in Sydney at an early age. He contrived to annoy the Australian racing authorities and was quick to accept Pierre Wertheimer's offer to ride for him in Paris in 1932. He was an immediate success, gaining the nickname 'Le Crocodile' for his habit of trying to win his races from behind. In 1934 Johnstone was taken on by Lord Glanely as stable jockey, but he then failed to win the Derby on Colombo and in June he was back at Chantilly riding for Wertheimer. The next year he won the One Thousand Guineas at Newmarket on Mesa; but he left Epsom despondently that June, having again achieved what many held to be impossible – getting Mesa beaten in the Oaks.

Johnstone was the most sophisticated of jockeys and a dedicated gambler. He often used to play cards with those he rode for, in the casino in Deauville, regularly attending the same night-clubs as the most cosmopolitan of *turfistes*. He had the rare gift of being able to tell how good a horse was just by riding it in a gallop; this, coupled with the fact that he spent a large part of his life studying the form book, meant that he was in a position to be a big gambler. He was never dishonest and would pull a horse – that is, try not to win – only if he was told to by its trainer. He often rode great races to beat his own money, which, with his taste for the high life, is probably why when he died an old friend had to give 1,000 francs to the estate, to bring it up to zero.

Frank Vogel, who used to place Johnstone's bets for him (it was a serious offence for jockeys to be caught betting), remembers being told to put 10,000 francs on the favourite in a race in which he was riding. He agreed to do so, but warned Rae to cover himself on his own mount. This had once been a good horse and, although it had shown no form recently, Frank thought it was coming back to its best and might be an outsider. There were no stalls in those days, and Johnstone managed to get to the rails early on in the race, where he stayed the whole way round; miraculously a series of gaps opened up for him and he stormed through, to catch the favourite on the line. When Johnstone had calmed down and they were on their way back to Paris, Vogel said that he had been proved right, he should have had a saver on his own horse. Johnstone told him not to be so absurd; his horse had had no chance, it was just a fluke he had got such a run on the inside, otherwise he would have been well beaten.

On the way to Vincennes one day, Johnstone said he was riding a difficult horse in the big race and he planned to be last when they turned into the straight, but he would go on to win. Vogel told him not to be foolish, for the run-in at Vincennes was too short and too uphill for him to have any chance if he rode that way. When the race came, Johnstone was last as they turned into the straight; although he flew up the hill, he could not catch the leader and finished second. On the way back to Paris, Vogel said that he should have won, for he had left himself too much ground to make up in the straight. Johnstone told him that if he had not been last coming into the straight, he would never have got as close as second.

After the war, Johnstone had the chance to show the English that he was a great jockey. He rode three Derby winners and three Oaks winners on the track that he was not supposed to be up to. In 1950 he rode four of the five English classic winners, as well as the winners of the 'Jockey Club' and the Irish Oaks. He retired from riding in 1957, showing himself to be a competent trainer, before collapsing and dying in Frank Vogel's arms in the weighing room at Le Tremblay in 1964.

Frank Vogel has been a familiar sight on French racecourses since the last war. He was the first Allied officer into Paris in 1944, immediately liberating Longchamp. He was awarded the Croix de Guerre, but he seemed to have forgotten this until an English magazine alluded to it. Although he has lived in Paris ever since, his accent is still as American as his belted fawn mackintosh and dark trilby. He has always been a friend of the trainer Alec Head's, and in the years after the war they made a regular income by sending good class French horses to run in selling races at Newmarket. The preparations for this gamble were thorough: the horse in question was always sent to a small provincial trainer a few weeks beforehand, to ensure that not even the French at Newmarket would have heard of the trainer on the race card.

The greatest gambling win of Vogel's career came one year when things were going so badly that he decided to have one last bet in June, before retiring for the season if it lost. He owed one million francs to the man who placed his bets for him in Paris, so he prepared a horse of his for a race on 'Grand Prix' day and staked enough on it at five to one – the price he expected to be returned – to clear his debt. Vogel spent the whole day telling anyone who asked him that his horse had no chance in the last race. The horse came off just the better in a sustained duel and won by a short head. When Vogel went to find out the odds he learnt that there had been a power cut and the Paris Mutuel, the French tote, had not taken account of his bet, so the winner was returned at fifty to one. 'No one has ever believed I did not pay someone to pull the plug out – I was so excited that I drove home and went straight to bed!'

Alec Head was the brilliant young man Aly Khan took on as his trainer in 1952, in the hope of reviving his fortunes on the turf. He began training in 1947, the same year he rode Le Paillon to come second in the champion hurdle at Cheltenham. Le Paillon, who was trained by his father William Head, went on to win that year's Prix de l'Arc de Triomphe. Head was only twenty-eight when in 1952 he trained his first 'Arc' winner, Nuccio, for the Aga Khan. Although

Aly Khan had few good horses at this stage, they became the closest of friends. He won the 1956 Derby with Lavandin for his other patron Pierre Wertheimer.

The present Aga Khan upset many old loyalties by removing from Alec Head's stables all the horses he inherited from his father, and placing them under the care of François Mathet.

Besides being a brilliant trainer, Alec Head was one of the first men to understand that top class stallions were going to become valuable commodities. He syndicated the last good horse the third Aga Khan bred, Charlottesville – who won the 'Jockey Club' and the 'Grand Prix' in the months following Aly Khan's death – for such a large sum that three of his owners removed their horses from his care, saying he was taking commercialism too far.

He was also one of the first Europeans to realize that the best racehorses were being bred in the United States. Together with Tim Rogers he made up the European attendance at the November 1969 Keeneland Sales. Head bought a Never Bend colt and Rogers a Northern Dancer, whom Head later bought when he was resold as a yearling at Newmarket in 1970. The first was Riverman and the second Lyphard; besides being excellent racehorses, they collected four French sires' championships between them from 1978 to 1981, when they were sold and returned to the United States. Riverman, whom Head paid $41,000 for on behalf of Mme Pierre Wertheimer, was syndicated in 1980 for $118 million.

Today, Alec Head and his partner, le Comte Roland de Chambure, own a 300-acre farm next door to one of the leading Kentucky stallion farms, Gainesway, where they keep many of their broodmares. They also own the Harras d'Etreham in Normandy. Head has recently been advised to relax a little, and his daughter Christianne, who is known as 'Criquette', has taken over some of the horses. Her father is still a frequent visitor to the stables. Head's son, Freddie, rides most of the family's horses.

In the 1940s and 1950s the pre-eminent French race was the Grand Prix de Paris, run at Longchamp at the end of June. My Love and Phil Drake were two Epsom Derby winners to complete the double. Every year many English racing enthusiasts and socialites would go over, and Aly Khan would always give a spectacular Grand Prix Ball at the Pré Catalan in the Bois de Boulogne. Deauville was the other social meeting, centred on a month of racing at Deauville and nearby Clairefontaine, an international polo tournament, and the casino.

The continued success of the French stables led the English to search for possible explanations. The Aga Khan, before he left for France himself, gave speeches on why the French won all the big races, and he was far from alone in addressing the subject. William Hill and Phil Bull of *Timeform* came to the conclusion that part of the reason was too strong an emphasis on two-year-old racing in Britain, which meant that the most attractive animal commercially was a precocious two-year-old, likely to win over five and six furlongs.

In the hope of encouraging British breeders to produce horses that might beat the French as three-year-olds, the Jockey Club increased the number of two-year-old races run over seven furlongs and a mile. Phil Bull instituted the Timeform Gold Cup, a valuable race for two-year-olds run over a mile that has now become the William Hill Futurity. Both were irrelevancies, as such races are won more often than not by two-year-olds that happen to be particularly mature, and many of them fail to train on, or fail to stay further than a mile anyway. Two-year-olds are today as commercially attractive as ever before, and more two-year-old champions fail to train on than ever before, although no one seems to mind about the lack of horses capable of staying a mile and a half.

Part of the reason for the successes of the French, besides the advantage of being able to continue racing uninterrupted for most of the Second World War, was the superiority of the French racing management. Perhaps the only technical field in which Britain could claim to lead France after the war was veterinary science. With such innovations as starting stalls, watering systems, and photo finishes, Britain was years behind.

The first demonstration of starting stalls in Newmarket was organized by Sir Robin McAlpine, who had long owned them in order to teach his horses how to jump out of them before sending them to race in France. The Duke of Norfolk announced beforehand that he would fight never to have them on an English racecourse, and after the demonstration he still did not like them, declaring that he was against the mechanization of animals. Reporting this the following morning in the *Daily Express*, Clive Graham wrote that he therefore presumed all the Arundel cows were still milked by hand.

In the 1950s Sir Robin McAlpine was part of a Jockey Club delegation sent to Longchamp in order to look at racecourse watering systems, with a view to installing them on selected racecourses in Britain. To their embarrassment, they were shown a pumping station
built in 1880.

For those who considered France to be the 'promised land' of racing, the most obvious explanation was that in France there were no
bookmakers. Most of the money the racing authorities of both
countries hand out comes from the money lost by those who bet on
horses. In Britain most of this money is retained by the bookmakers, whereas all legal betting in France is done on the Paris Mutuel,
the state-owned totalizator. The proceeds are then divided between
the French government and the Société d'Encouragement, with the
result that prize money in France has always been comparatively
higher and racecourse facilities more modern, and the Société has
been able to introduce such schemes as giving additional prize
money to winners bred in France.

For a time after the mid 1960s English envy of the French system
diminished, due to the appearance of two English-owned and -bred
champions – Royal Palace and Brigadier Gerard – and because it was
now apparent that American-bred horses posed the greatest threat
in the long run. Nevertheless, until the middle 1970s racing in
France was superior to that in Britain. It has never been a large entertainment industry in France; it is rather the pastime of a national and
cosmopolitan élite, subsidized and supervised by French governments keen to promote an activity that is a lucrative source of public
funds. The French racing administration, and many of those who
own and train horses there, have a far better record of innovating
and changing with the times than their British counterparts do. To
appreciate the truth of this, let us consider the state of racing in Britain during the 1950s and 1960s.

7

The Challenge of Change

Many of the best racehorses trained in England during the 1950s and 1960s were owned and bred by wealthy men who could afford to treat racing as a sport. In 1953 the fourteen owners who won the most prize money all relied upon horses they had bred themselves. Many of these patrons came from families with a tradition of involvement with racing, but there were also representatives of new money – businessmen and industrialists – and a growing number of foreigners attracted to English racing by its glamour and historical standing.

One of the first of the foreigners to make his mark on English racing was the Gaekwar of Baroda. He took on the twenty-one-year-old Mrs Peter Nelson as his adviser, having been impressed by her ability to reel off any pedigree to four generations – also, no doubt, by her charm. He bought the Warren Place stables in Newmarket and founded the Baroda Stud in Ireland, before going to the yearling sales in 1945 and causing a sensation by buying Sayajirao, a full brother to the Derby winner Dante, for 28,000 guineas. This was the highest price ever paid for a yearling in Europe and was not surpassed until 1966.

Sayajirao was a success, winning the St Leger and other good races, and for five years the Gaekwar of Baroda was regularly to be seen at Epsom, Ascot, and Deauville. In 1951 political changes in India led to his deposition and relative impoverishment, so he was forced to sell his horses and join the ranks of the general public.

Sir Victor Sassoon was a more lasting influence on British racing. He bought his first horses in England in 1925, and was a frequent and extravagant visitor to bloodstock sales for the remainder of his life. In his last eight years his perseverance was repaid famously, as he won the Derby four times with Pinza, Hard Ridden, Crepello, and St Paddy, breeding the later two also. At his death in 1961 he owned sixty-one broodmares, and studs in Newmarket, Yorkshire, and Ireland. Sassoon was always the benevolent patron, refusing offers from abroad for his stallions so that British breeders would not be deprived of their services, and even offering cheap nominations to breeders whom he considered to be worthy but not wealthy. He was never elected to the Jockey Club, presumably due to personal incompatibility. He could be pedantic with his jockeys, giving them strict instructions before a race and refusing to let them use a whip on his horses. He also managed to annoy his co-religionists by publicly announcing: 'There is one race greater than the Jewish race, and that's the Derby!'

From 1952 Sassoon's studs were managed by Noel Murless, who also trained two of his Derby winners for him. The first, Crepello, was an achievement as he was basically an unsound horse; his only appearances as a three-year-old were in the Two Thousand Guineas and the Derby, both of which he won. The second, St Paddy, was the produce of a mare Murless had bought for Sassoon.

Later knighted for his services to racing, Murless is the outstanding post-war English trainer. Between 1948 and 1973 he trained the winners of nineteen classic races and was the champion trainer nine times. He started training in Yorkshire before the war, after spending five years working for Hubert Hartigan in Ireland and having been a professional jump jockey. He took over from Fred Darling at Beckhampton in 1947, but he stayed for only five seasons as he never liked the place, considering it to be uneconomic. He moved to Warren Place at Newmarket, where he stayed until 1976, when he handed it over to his son-in-law, Henry Cecil.

Murless is said to have been a poor judge of a yearling, but once he had a two-year-old in training he had an extraordinary ability to tell how good it was going to be. As a result, his classic horses had their entire careers planned before they had seen the racecourse. John Hislop remembers being told by Murless that a filly of his would win the Oaks, in the February of her two-year-old days. She did not, because on the day of the race she was in season and finished only fourth, but she won the Cheshire Oaks and other good races. Murless was lucky to train for very rich men who bred much of their own stock, like Stanhope and Jim Joel, Aly Khan, George A. Pope, and Lord Howard de Walden, as well as Sir Victor Sassoon. However, since he started in such a humble fashion, this reflected upon his skill and character, rather than on his luck. He possesses, to a marked degree, the attribute most important for the trainer: a natural empathy with horses. Lord Howard de Walden says that he had the ability to walk into a fractious horse's box and make it relax, just by being there.

Noel Murless took on the nineteen-year-old Lester Piggott as his stable jockey in 1955, and the partnership lasted until 1966. At the beginning of the season Murless and Piggott did not sign a formal contract, although up until June they both behaved as if they had. Piggott then announced he would ride Valoris in the Oaks, even though Murless was running Varinia and expected him, as stable jockey, to ride her. Valoris won the race easily with Piggott riding, and Murless was furious at what he saw as Piggott's disloyalty. He refused to let him ride his horses again until July, and arranged for the Australian jockey George Moore to ride for him the following year.

It was generally thought Piggott had acted foolishly and would be unable to maintain the same level of success as a freelance, but subsequent events proved the opposite to be true. Piggott's partnership with Vincent O'Brien, the trainer of Valoris, lasted ten years and enabled him to ride such great horses as Sir Ivor, Nijinsky, and Alleged. There are few jockeys with the stature and financial acumen of Lester Piggott; he showed it was possible for a jockey to be independent of any binding contracts and still ride Derby winners and be champion jockey.

The many sentimentalists in the racing world enjoyed the fact that in Noel Murless's last season, 1976, when he trained the brilliant two-year-old J. O. Tobin for George Pope, his old relationship with Piggott was renewed. Murless was tempted to postpone retirement to train J. O. Tobin for a Derby confrontation with The Minstrel, but he decided against it, and the colt returned to the United States. He thinks J. O. Tobin would have won the Derby – as long as Piggott had ridden him, rather than The Minstrel.

More than one of Sir Noel Murless's owners has said that they have not really enjoyed owning horses since his retirement. He was perhaps the last old-fashioned trainer; a horseman, not a businessman. He had no need to attend bloodstock sales throughout the world, he did not have 150 or more horses in his care, and he trained for rich, knowledgeable, and experienced patrons of racing. Not surprisingly many of his owners saw him as a friend rather than a business partner. So closely did he fulfil this role that by the end of his career he had become something of an anachronism. The aims of a modern trainer, the skills he requires, and even his daily routine are very different.

While British horse-racing remained, for some, the sport it had seemingly always been, pressures were afoot that would transform it into one facet of an international business. How would those who were responsible for administering racing face up to and cope with the changes and challenges of the post-war decades? Like many other lasting English institutions, the Jockey Club gained its power by default – relying upon the assumption by its members that they had the right to dictate to others, who would willingly acquiesce to that authority. For much of its existence the Jockey Club has had unquestioned authority in the racing world, holding direct responsibility for the livelihood of all licensed trainers, jockeys, and stable lads, who could be banned upon private decision and without appeal. Only the need to maintain the goodwill of the racing world curbed its power. In 1970, when the Club felt its authority to be under threat, it was incorporated by a Royal Charter that recognized its authority and declared it could by modified only by an Act of Parliament.

According to R. Black, the Jockey Club 'seems to have been started for the express purpose of knitting together men of like class and pursuits and keeping at arm's length men of different class, though of like pursuits'.[1] The existence of the Jockey Club is first recorded in 1752, and it did not waver from this purpose for 200 years. The Club has around 120 members; it is run by six stewards, elected for a three-year term, one of whom is appointed senior steward. Elections and the appointment of stewards are determined by a procedure similar to that of 'Pop' at Eton, the self-electing body that acts as prefects there. The serving stewards draw up a shortlist, upon which the remaining members vote, so a small group exert a strong influence upon all decisions. Not surprisingly such a structure has produced a bias towards conformists and those with a more traditional approach.

Only recently has the Club been forced to consider a purpose for

teve Donoghue and
rown Jack (*W.W. Rouch*)

Charlie Smirke the year
he won the Derby on the
Maharaja of Rajpipla's
Windsor Lad (*W.W. Rouch*)

(*Overleaf*) Arriving for
the Royal meeting,
Ascot station, 1936
(*Topham*)

bove) Marcel Boussac ds in Talma II and e Johnstone after they d won the 1951 St Leger *pperfoto*)

eft) Marcel Boussac's ng at Chantilly. Rae nstone (centre with dkerchief) talks to ussac's trainer Charles nblat (with binoculars) d others (*Popperfoto*)

ght) The connections Pinza shortly after his rby victory. *Left to t*: Sir Victor Sassoon, rman Bertie, Gordon hards (*Popperfoto*)

Noel Murless and Aly Khan at Epsom before Tulyar's Derby, 1952 (*Popperfoto*

Aly Khan with Petite Etoile and Lester Piggott after they had won
the 1959 Oaks (*Popperfoto*)

The Begum and Aga Khan at Epsom in June 1938 (*Popperfoto*)

Nasrullah, champion sire in Great Britain and the United States and sire of the winners of 906 races (*W.W. Rouch*)

racing other than the enjoyment of its own members and a rather nebulous idea of the well-being of the thoroughbred. The Club saw the racing world as a group of people who shared similar pleasures; their role was to exercise a minimum of regulation in order to allow those people to pursue their own pleasure. The idea of defining the purpose of horse-racing and then attempting to direct its development so that this purpose was fulfilled was never considered. In France, by contrast, the post of director-general of the Société d'Encouragement, filled for many years by Jean Rommanet, was created to provide a comprehensive means for the development of the industry, under the supervision of one man. As early as 1870 one of its members, Sir Joseph Hawley, suggested the Jockey Club should broaden its membership basis. No immediate action was taken, and at one stage between the two world wars there were only two commoners among its members.

In 1941 Lord Ilchester, then senior steward, set up a Jockey Club committee to consider 'the whole future of racing in general, with particular reference to the encouragement of owners and greater comfort and convenience of the public'. The committee reported in 1943, acknowledging that, if there was not immediate action, British racing would continue its steady decline:

> The attractiveness of racing in England has fallen far behind that in the countries in which it is of more recent origin, from the point of view of the general public as distinct from the regular racegoer.

It was perhaps this report that caused Lord Derby and George Lambton to worry about the future of racing and the English upper classes. But they need not have worried, for after the war the Ilchester Report was quietly forgotten about and the Club assumed its traditional role, under the leadership of the seventh Earl of Sefton, the sixth Earl of Rosebery, and the sixteenth Duke of Norfolk.

Newmarket has always been the home of the Jockey Club. The pious attitude of its members towards the racecourses there has caused a great deal of ill feeling. Until the 1950s it was not possible to buy a badge for the members' enclosure without getting a voucher signed by two members of the Club; no exceptions were made, even for trainers.

Major Peter Nelson once attempted to enter the members' enclosure after saddling a runner. He refused to take no for an answer and demanded to see Lord Sefton, who was then the senior steward. Lord Sefton arrived, apparently unaware such a rule existed, and took Major Nelson into the stand, saying that it was a silly rule and he would see about getting it changed. The Newmarket gatemen were renowned for the conscientious manner in which they upheld such regulations. A racing journalist remembers that his wife and children were unable to enter the stand, even at the end of a day's racing, to join him on the walk to the car park. Such incidents may have been trivial, but they helped to sully the Jockey Club's reputation.

The Duke of Norfolk was appointed His Majesty's Representative at Ascot in 1945, running it until 1972. Under his rule the King George VI and Queen Elizabeth II Stakes was founded, becoming the first £100,000 race in England: it is now established as one of Europe's great races. Two new grandstands were built and, although they provide magnificent facilities for those in the members' enclosure, they cannot be said to have contributed much to the benefit of the ordinary race-goer – as anyone who has fought their way through the tunnel between the grandstand and the paddock during the Royal meeting will confirm.

When the plans for a new stand at the Newmarket 'Rowley Mile Course' were under discussion in the 1960s, Sir Robin McAlpine put forward the radical idea of segregating the various enclosures by having them on different levels. His plan was to build a stand with the winning post facing the middle of the stand, rather than the members' enclosure, so that those in every enclosure could stand in line with the winning post. The Silver Ring, the cheapest enclosure, would be on the top floor, the Tattersall's one down, and the members' on the first floor and lawn. The paddock would be on the far side of the course, so that everyone could see it. There would be a tunnel under the course to reach it. Not surprisingly, he was unable to secure the approval of the Duke of Norfolk, and the final meeting of decision was held whilst Sir Robin McAlpine was on holiday.

Some of the more persistent critics of the Jockey Club believe it is unfortunate for racing that there is no longer a figure like the sixth Earl of Rosebery amongst the Club's members. This is not because they feel a repeat of some of Lord Rosebery's preposterous remarks would bring about the Club's demise, but because Lord Rosebery had the self-confidence and stature to hector anyone if he thought it might be for the benefit of racing. Although at times he was arrogant to the point of absurdity, Lord Rosebery eventually gained the respect of most of his opponents. For twenty-five years he played a prominent role in racing, being senior steward in 1932 and 1948 and president of the Thoroughbred Breeders' Association from 1932 to 1956. Until his death in 1974, at the age of ninety-two, he was indeed racing's elder statesman.

As a young man Lord Rosebery was a distinguished sportsman. He was of international standard as a polo player, and he captained Surrey in the days when county cricket teams were required to have a 'gentleman' in command. For some time he managed to combine this responsibility with being the Liberal Member of Parliament for Edinburgh. He was elected to the Jockey Club in 1924, although he did not come into his own as an owner until he inherited the Mentmore Stud from his father in 1929. Something had happened during Rosebery's youth which prevented him from being universally popular, and Lord Howard de Walden resigned from the Club in protest at his election. It was also noticed that Lord Dalmeny, as he then was, was never invited to dine with his father.

There are various possible explanations for these anomalies, although Rosebery never divulged the truth. He was somehow involved in a famous racing scandal of 1906. In October of that year there was a match at Sandown Park between Pitchbattle and Piari. Piari was owned and ridden by Lord Gerard, a godson of King Edward VII, not renowned for his intelligence. Pitchbattle was owned and ridden by Hugh de Wend Fenton, and was much the faster horse. As would be expected, when betting on the race started Pitchbattle was the favourite, at long odds on, but astonishingly there seemed to be more money for Piari and it was he who started favourite. Piari then proceeded to win the race, although it was noticed that de Wend Fenton made remarkably little effort to win. An observer later reported that 'the silly bugger was so cocksure that he pulled the horse up in front of the stewards, rather than putting him to sleep down the back straight, as anyone else would have done'.

As a result of the race, de Wend Fenton was warned off the turf, Lord Gerard sold all his horses and retired voluntarily in shame. Many people connected de Wend Fenton with Lord Dalmeny, which cannot have pleased his father, who besides being a member of the Jockey Club had also been Prime Minister. Many years later a frequent guest of Lord Rosebery's, fortified by quantities of his lordship's finest champagne, asked him what the true story of the 'Pitchbattle case' was. Lord Rosebery replied that certain people had gone to his father to ask for leniency on behalf of de Wend Fenton; so it was thought that he was involved.

There were more unfavourable rumours circulating about Lord Dalmeny after the controversial 1913 Derby. In the race the favourite, Craganour, just managed to beat the 100-to-1 outsider, Aboyeur. The story runs that soon after the race Dalmeny talked to his father, who was acting as a steward that day (although not on the Derby, as he had had a runner himself); and having learnt that it was unlikely Craganour would be allowed to keep the race, Dalmeny then proceeded to wage large sums of money on Aboyeur being awarded the race in the stewards' room. It is impossible to say what Lord Rosebery told his son, but Craganour was disqualified, the race was awarded to Aboyeur, and Dalmeny won a large sum of money.

Lord Rosebery had his own convictions as to his position in society. During a visit to London he was approached by Hudson, the Minister of Agriculture, who told him that after making some inquiries into farming in Scotland he had decided something needed to be changed on Lord Rosebery's estates. Lord Rosebery replied that he would run his estates how he wanted, adding: 'My ancestors were farming while yours were blowing bubbles!' – a reference to Hudson's family, who had made their money from the manufacture of soap. He was once asked what he thought of a proposal to elect Lord Manton – the present senior steward's grandfather – to the Jockey Club; he is said to have replied that, in his opinion, it would be wiser to wait a generation.

Rosebery did not take kindly to criticism in the press. Clive Graham once wrote in his column in the *Daily Express* that the form book should be printed in Braille for the benefit of the stewards. Rosebery retaliated by telephoning Lord Beaverbrook and demanding that he look for a new racing correspondent. Beaverbrook politely declined to do so.

After the Second World War there was a heated debate on the subject of the decline of British breeding. Much of the blame for this state of affairs was placed on the Aga Khan for selling his Derby winners for export. In 1945 Lord Rosebery proudly announced he had turned down offers from abroad for his colt Midas, who had finished second in that year's Derby, and he would stand the horse in England. Midas may have been a good racehorse but he was not a particularly sound one. Tom Nickals wrote a piece in the *Sporting Life* saying that it was all very well saving Midas for British breeders, but how many of them would be pleased when they had had a closer look at his forelegs? Nickals had been given a job by Tattersall's, the bloodstock auctioneers, due to start later that year. After the article appeared, he was summoned to a general meeting of Tattersall's at the Rutland Arms in Newmarket; Gerald Deane asked him if he had written the article and, when he affirmed he had, Deane informed him that in that case Tattersall's had no interest in employing him.

Nickals went up to Lord Rosebery in the unsaddling enclosure at Newmarket, and had the courage to tell him that he considered he had behaved in an ungentlemanly fashion, ruining his chance of employment. Rosebery refused to acknowledge his existence for the next two years, but then started to talk to him again and eventually invited him to tea at Mentmore.

During the years Lord Rosebery ran the turf, it was not only journalists who were wary of criticizing him. It seems there were few outside his circle of friends who approached him with any confidence. He was a large man physically and skilled at putting people down: he used to announce with pride that he was 'half Scottish and half Jewish; mean and unpleasant on both sides'. He is said to have brought to a close a meeting of the Jockey Club – called to discuss some proposal for the benefit of the public – by standing and banging on the table to emphasize: 'The public don't count!'

It is a matter of embarrassment to some members of the Jockey Club today that many of its employees, its handicappers, and other skilled officials, are paid small salaries. It was Admiral Rous who said the perfect public handicapper was harder to find than a Prime Minister:

> I might pick out three Prime Ministers who would satisfy the public, but I can discover no man gifted with the qualifications of the hand-icapper. We want a man like Caesar's wife, above suspicion, of independent means, a perfect knowledge of the form and actual condition

of every public horse, without having the slightest interest in any stable.

Rous must have been flattered when he was himself appointed
public handicapper in 1855 – which is perhaps the origin of the belief
in handicappers needing no payment. This was Lord Rosebery's
opinion: he considered it a privilege to work for the Jockey Club
and he expected the same loyalty and respect from the Club's
employees that he was given by his own servants. If Rosebery was
never well liked, it is improbable he ever wanted to be, but he was
respected by many in the racing world.

One of the reforms Rosebery instigated was taking on professionals, known as stewards' secretaries, to help local stewards carry out
their duties. Local stewards were notoriously inefficient, one of the
more infamous being Captain Mark Weyland. The stewards'
enquiry into the result of a race on which he was officiating once had
to be delayed because Weyland had disappeared. He was finally
found in the bookmakers' ring, betting on the result of the enquiry
he was to hold.

Relying upon part-time, amateur stewards worked effectively
only when there were enough men and women who had the time
and money to go racing regularly. To carry out the duties of a steward it is necessary to be able to 'read' a race properly; that is, to
watch a race and take in exactly what happened to each horse. Those
who write the comments in the form book and *Raceform Notebook*
rarely need to watch a television replay before making notes as to the
position of each horse throughout the race – and it is well known
that even the best-situated camera distorts the perspective. This skill
ins the result of many years' practice, and few people whose profession is not in racing acquire such experience today. Many local stewards are retired people, or businessmen taking a day off, and few of
them have had the leisure to acquire such skills.

The Jockey Club was forced to make the first real concessions to
the changing political climate when it became clear that British racing was in need of money. The level of prize money had fallen far
behind that on offer in France, and the amenities on British
racecourses were horrendous. New grandstands were needed,
as well as technical improvements such as photo finishes, patrol
cameras, and public address systems. It had been hoped that the set-

ting up of the Horserace Totalisator Board in 1929 would provide the needed funds, but the Tote has always suffered from unimaginative management, unable to change the habits of a betting public well used to bookmakers. It was even suggested in the 1970s that the Tote should be privatized and handed over to the big four bookmaking firms.

The solution to the sport's lack of funds was a deal between the government, the bookmakers, and the Jockey Club. The 1960 Betting and Gaming Act legalized betting away from racecourses, gave the government revenue from betting tax, and set up the Horserace Betting Levy Board, to collect contributions from bookmakers and the Tote, for the purpose of improving horse-racing, breeding, and veterinary science. Until then it had been illegal to bet outside a racecourse, except for those who possessed credit accounts with established bookmakers. It goes without saying that only those who were well off and 'respectable' were given credit facilities, so the majority of the public were committing an offence every time they had a bet. This had had little effect on the volume of betting, and there were numerous street bookmakers. In 1960 there were twenty such illegal bookmakers in York alone, some of whom had been at the same address for over twenty years.

British politicians have always been reluctant to have anything to do with horse-racing. Those on the political left have tended to regard it as an obscene pastime for the very rich, whilst many Conservatives regard betting as immoral and horse-racing as the indulgence of degenerate members of the aristocracy and working classes. A steward of the Jockey Club once asked Harold Wilson if he would like to attend the Derby, only to be interrupted by Mary Wilson, who assured him: 'Harold and I never bet.' The Jockey Club have also tried to persuade Mrs Thatcher to take luncheon with them – without, as yet, any success. As Lord Gowrie, the Minister for the Arts, explained on a visit to the National Horseracing Museum, Mrs Thatcher does not really approve.

The result of this reluctance, coupled with the Jockey Club's determination to avoid any outside interference in racing unless absolutely necessary, has been that government intervention in racing has been mistimed and inept. The parliamentary debates on the Betting and Gaming Act were marked by an almost complete ignorance of racing displayed by those taking part, with the exception of

George Wigg and Richard Stanley. When betting was legalized the restrictions placed upon betting-shop owners did not allow them to provide even the minimum of amenities that might have prevented squalidity. It was left to the unlikely figure of Sir Ian Gilmour to sponsor a Bill in 1984 allowing betting-shop owners to provide comfortable chairs and light refreshments for their customers.

The Levy Board was, in theory, a challenge to the Jockey Club's authority, as the Levy comprised almost the total sum of money spent on the administration of racing. The Jockey Club nominates two members of the Board, but these do not constitute a majority, and the chairman is appointed by the Home Secretary. After a stormy period, when George Wigg was Chairman of the Levy Board, the two institutions have come to hold harmonious views on how the money should be spent. Wigg was retired from the House of Commons and created a life peer when his strenuous efforts to uncover such scandals as the 'Profumo affair' failed to earn him more than a grudging admiration, even from his own Labour benches. In 1967 Harold Wilson appointed him chairman of the Levy Board, but although his dynamism enabled him to secure more funds for racing, he was never diplomatic in dealing with those who had a vested interest in the Board's affairs.

When he took over the post from Field-Marshal Lord Harding, Wigg was summoned to a Jockey Club meeting and told it was his job to collect the money to give to the Club to spend. His reply was fairly rude. Since Wigg left the Board in 1972, it has rarely been involved in any publicized rows. The immediate effect of the extra funds supplied by the Levy was an increase in the level of prize money. The winner's prize money for the Derby was doubled between 1963 and 1964, and the 1964 Derby was the most valuable ever. The £72,000 J. Ismay received that year after Santa Claus's victory was equivalent to £450,000 twenty years later.

The other challenge to the Jockey Club during the post-war decades came from the pressure groups that various factions in the racing world organized. The first to be formed was the Thoroughbred Breeders' Association; followed, in 1945, by the Racehorse Owners' Association, and later by such organizations as the National Trainers' Federation and the Jockeys' Association of Great Britain. The Jockey Club was wary of such organizations, partly because it thought them to be faintly absurd – after all, the

Jockey Club is the original owners' association and had the power to deflate the later bodies simply by removing the licence of any trouble-makers. The Club also feared that a proliferation of pressure groups would lead to a multitude of conflicting voices, each purporting to be speaking for racing. That the formation of these organizations may have been symptomatic of the gulf between the amateurs who administered racing and the professionals who participated in it does not seem to have occurred to the Jockey Club.

The Club responded to the challenge largely by seeming to ignore its existence and applying hidden sanctions. J. V. Rank, a lavish supporter of racing for thirty years, was not elected to the Jockey Club until he was sixty-nine, perhaps because he was one of the founding members of the Racehorse Owners' Association. The most effective of these organizations were those representing the bookmakers, and it was the result of their skilful lobbying of Parliament that the question of a Tote monopoly was not even raised in the discussions prior to the passing of the Betting and Gaming Act. The position was succinctly summed up by owner-breeder David Robinson in his speech to the Gimcrack Dinner in 1969:

> It is nonsense to argue, as some do, that business and sport cannot mix. In another age racing may have been purely a sport. But for a long time now it has been an industry, and as an industry it has declined because the administrators of racing have had neither the business experience to run it effectively, nor apparently the will, or even the desire, to bring in that experience for the benefit of racing.

The evidence of racing being a business, and a badly administered one, should have been clear to anyone. One of the most damaging consequences of this mismanagement was the leeway given to the criminal element in the racing world. The Racecourse Security Services were so amateurish that only the most obvious cases of the use of stimulants or sedatives were detected. To avoid detection it was necessary only to find some means of administering the drug other than with a hypodermic syringe. There were those who claimed certain French horses were doped to go faster, but more serious were the wilfully inflicted setbacks incurred by a number of ante-post favourites for big races. Alcide was heavily backed for the 1958 Derby after winning the Lingfield Derby Trial by twelve lengths:

eight days later he was found in his box with a large lump on his back ribs; closer examination revealed a broken rib and he was unable to run for three months, although he recovered in time to win the St Leger. A similar injury befell Pinturischo, the ante-post favourite for the 1961 Derby, except that his injury was so severe he was never able to run again.

If a bookmaker knows that the ante-post favourite for the Derby will not be able to run in it, he is in a position to make a lot of money. There is betting on the Derby for six months or more prior to the race, and any bet placed on a horse that does not run is immediately forfeited. If a bookmaker was sure that a certain well-fancied horse would be a non-runner, he would only have to offer slightly better odds than his rivals to take a great deal of money on the horse. One of the arguments in favour of a Tote monopoly is that, without bookmakers, the temptations of this sort of malpractice would be greatly reduced.

As we have seen, then, David Robinson was correct to say racing had long since ceased to be purely a sport. The gradual pace of change has accelerated dramatically since the early 1970s. Before considering how these changes have affected those in the racing world, let us examine international developments in the bloodstock market. By the middle 1970s the value of bloodstock in Europe was rising rapidly in real terms, and this was partly the consequence of events in the United States. We should also clarify this distinction between 'business' and 'sport': to call racing a business is to say it involves an exchange between buyers and sellers, and it is far from clear what end product those who are in the racing world are trying to exchange.

8

The Business of Horse-racing

The business of horse-racing has always consisted of two distinct, related activities. Firstly, racing has long been an entertainment, which is its primary justification. The other business is the breeding, buying, and selling of thoroughbred racehorses. Neither of these two activities could exist without the other, yet they each demand different requirements from the horse itself. Many of the problems of the racing world today are the result of the divergence of the demands each side of the industry makes upon the racehorse. For horse-racing to be entertaining it must be competitive, and yet the commercialization of the bloodstock industry has reached such a peak that it encourages the very opposite.

In 1953 Lord Rosebery complained that the capital value of a good three-year-old was too great to justify keeping it in training for another season. Now it seems that the capital value of a horse who has won a single major race is too great to justify keeping it in training. The entertainment industry demands racehorses who are robust and consistent; it requires the superior members of each equine generation to take each other on, over a variety of distances, for a period of two or three years. The bloodstock industry, however, encourages the production of precocious animals, and provides huge financial incentives for the owner of a superior animal to avoid taking on his competitors, once his horse has gained a reputation. As has been explained, racing has always been a business, but this has become a matter for comment only when the two branches of the business appear to be pursuing contradictory ends. The racehorse has always been a symbol of power and beauty, but today the perspective of the bloodstock industry is transforming the horse into purely a power tool: a valuable commodity, conferring some social accolade.

Horse-racing provides entertainment both as a medium on which to gamble, and as a spectacle to enjoy for its own sake. Originally this entertainment was restricted to those who actively participated in the sport. This was the form racing took in the seventeenth century; men raced horses to settle private wagers or challenges, often riding their own charges. Yet racing soon acquired a popular following; when the first recorded handicap was run – the Oaklands Stakes at Ascot in 1791 – a crowd of 40,000 turned up to watch.

Until the middle of the nineteenth century this popular following was not something those who administered racing saw any need to encourage – indeed, it was a side effect some, like Admiral Rous, found distasteful – but from then onwards it came to be seen as a useful source of revenue. Sandown Park, which opened in 1875, was the first racecourse to be fully enclosed and to charge an admission fee to every part of the course. The income the course received was sufficient to enable it to stage the first race with £10,000 in prize money in this country (the equivalent of around £300,000 today), when it inaugurated the Eclipse Stakes in 1886.

From this time until the formation of the Horserace Betting Levy Board in 1961, with the exception of a few sponsored races, all prize money was made up of the contributions of racecourses and the contributions of owners, through entry fees. Thus it was essential to provide good sport at a reasonable cost, for the level of prize money depended upon the size of attendances.

As we have seen, the Levy was a response to the pressing need for more funds, in order to allow British breeding to remain internationally competitive, to attract foreign money into British racing, and to maintain the employment of the 100,000 people who relied upon the industry for their livelihood, so from 1961 it has been in the interests of all those in the racing world to maximize the betting turnover. For this reason there are now at least two race meetings on every day of the year, except for Sundays, Good Friday, and three days over Christmas. This was one of Lord Wigg's ideas; he reasoned that the man in the betting shop would be tempted to wager more if there was a race every quarter of an hour. Many mid-week meetings at small racecourses are far from profitable, and would not take place at all without the subsidies provided by the Levy Board.

The horserace betting turnover is in the region of £2,500 million, from which the Levy Board receives a little more than £20 million annually. The total amount of prize money on offer, for both flat and National Hunt racing, is about £20 million. Of this, £10 million are supplied by the Levy Board, £4 million by the sponsors, and the remaining £6 million are contributed by racecourses and owners' entry fees. The remaining £10 million of the Levy are spent on grants to racecourses to improve amenities, technical services, and so on. Clearly horse-racing does rely upon the Levy.

Over the last 150 years, racing has changed from being a private affair for the wealthy – in which those who participated as owners paid trainers, jockeys, stable lads, and farriers to provide them with both a spectacle and a medium on which to bet – to the more diverse industry of today. Horse-racing entertains those who own racehorses, those who attend race meetings, and those who bet on racing away from racecourses. Each of these groups contributes to the running costs of the industry; the owner pays training fees and for the services of the other professionals in the racing world; the race-goer pays to gain entrance to the racecourse; and the punter contributes indirectly through the Levy raised on the turnover of bookmakers and the Tote.

The bloodstock industry is distinct from this. Yet most of those who own racehorses, and all of those who breed them, look to the bloodstock industry to subsidize their indulgence. Only five per cent of racehorses in training in Britain earn enough prize money to cover the cost of keeping them. For the last 100 years, owners have looked to the bloodstock market to help finance their pastime. The recent dramatic increase in the value of the racehorse is only the culmination of a gradual process by which both the supply of and the demand for the superior racehorse have been freed from the restrictions that once bound them.

By the end of the nineteenth century, the commercialization of horse-racing was well advanced. In 1889 the Duke of Westminster sold Ormonde to an Argentinian breeder for £12,000 (the equivalent of over £300,000 today). The following year Baron Hirsch gave the equivalent of about £150,000 for the yearling filly he later named La Flèche, and at this time St Simon was standing at a fee of £500, the equivalent of more than £10,000 today. However, the growth of the bloodstock market was restricted by the hierarchical structure of both the racing world and the thoroughbred population.

At this time racehorses were born into one of five categories: they were either classic horses, good horses, handicap horses, sellers, or jumpers. Although there were many classically bred horses whose ability on the racecourse was not of the same exalted standard as their pedigree, few animals bred to be good horses or handicappers were able to belie their pedigree and win classic races. Nearly every equine generation included a few distinctive individuals, who were able not only to dominate their contemporaries on the racecourse, but could maintain their pre-eminence after they retired to stud. The most striking example of such an individual is St Simon, who was the leading stallion in Great Britain nine times in a period of ten years. There were only a few stallions and broodmares likely to produce a classic winner; and as most of the produce of this élite were retained by their breeders, the number of top class yearlings, stallions, and broodmares to be put up for auction was small.

The majority of leading owners of the nineteenth century looked upon racing as a sport. The pleasure of the sport was derived as much from breeding the best racehorses as from owning them. The number of broodmares likely to produce a classic winner was small enough for men like Lord Falmouth and the Duke of Westminster to own the majority of them at a particular time. Such men were prepared to pay large fees for the services of the best stallions, but as there were only one or two proven classic stallions and a handful of top class broodmares this did not create a thriving market.

A successful stallion was a lucrative source of income, but the primary reason all owners hoped to acquire one was to gain, through unlimited access, an advantage over their competitors. Similarly the overseas demand for British thoroughbreds – a quarter of the winners of the Derby in the nineteenth century were exported as stallions – was a welcome source of income, but not something any owner considered until the end of a horse's racing career. Thus those who owned racehorses did so for the pleasure of success on the racecourse and the challenge offered by breeding; if they were able to make money by selling their cast-offs abroad, or by allowing others to use their stallions, this was nothing more than a welcome bonus.

This situation began to change when the demand for racehorses became more competitive. The new men who came into racing from the end of the nineteenth century were not necessarily experts in the art of breeding the racehorse themselves, nor did they all possess the capital and patience required to found a successful stud. These new-comers created a demand for young horses who had the potential to win good races, and the first commercial breeders and bloodstock agents appeared in response to this demand. The British Bloodstock Agency was founded in 1911, and it was a sign of the expanding market that six of the winners of the Derby in the inter-war years had been sold as yearlings.

The gradual rise in the value of the best bloodstock over the last 100 years is the result of a greater and more varied demand. Like any other industry, the bloodstock industry is affected by outside economic influence, and there was a marked fall in the demand for racehorses during the economic depressions of the 1930s and early 1970s, as well as during both world wars. The more varied demand for racehorses led to the transformation in the typology of the racehorse described earlier with reference to Lord Derby's breeding operations. The commercial breeders responded to the new demand by producing more horses and by placing more emphasis on speed and precociousness. Once the best racehorses were descended from a few pre-eminent families and owned by the members of an heredit-ary, landowning élite; but by the 1980s there were, spread through-out the world, hundreds of stallions and broodmares each of whom was capable of producing a Derby winner. Thousands of possible classic winners were now sold as yearlings in salerooms worldwide.

A further factor in the expansion of the bloodstock market was the escalating cost of maintaining racehorses. The breeding and training of the racehorse are labour-intensive activities, and there has been a considerable real rise in wages, and thus in training fees, in the last sixty years. Alec Taylor, the leading trainer of the 1920s, charged £3.10s a week for each horse in his stable, the equivalent of around £50 a week today. Guy Harwood charges £180 a week. This has meant that the capital appreciation of a successful racehorse has become the means by which all owners have subsidized the luxury of spending money on horses. Even Lord Derby looked to the sale of nominations to his stallions, and the continual culling of his stud, to enable him to race on the scale he desired.

The existence of a flourishing bloodstock market was, initially, in the interest of all those in the racing world – except perhaps those who had once enjoyed protected access to the best blood. New

owners could go to the yearling sales with the hope of buying a
Derby winner and later look to the resale value of a successful
racehorse as a means of funding their next purchase. Ben Irish, a successful market gardener, bought Papyrus as a yearling; and when
Mid Day Sun won the 1937 Derby he was the only horse Mrs G. B.
Miller had in training at the time: neither would have had any chance
of being connected with a Derby winner 100 years before. The
breeding of racehorses was also opened up to new competition, as
there was now a thriving market for horses likely to win as two-
year-olds, as well as for classic horses, and the yearling sales provided a quick return on the initial capital outlay involved in buying
broodmares and rearing foals.

The less benevolent effects of this new commercialism were first
noticed before the First World War and became a matter for serious
concern in the 1930s. In a free international market for racehorses,
the monopoly of the best blood enjoyed by British breeders for 200
years was certain to be eroded. The United States soon became the
world's foremost breeding nation, and by the 1940s Britain was
ranked behind France as well. In more recent years Britain's breeding industry has declined still further, with Eire and Australia holding sound claims to a superior position in a hypothetical world table.
This was partly the result of Britain's relative economic decline, but
the reactionary outlook of Britain's racing administration, and the
social sanctions applied to those like the Aga Khan and David
Robinson who admitted applying business principles to the management of their racing affairs, contributed to the *malaise*.

As early as 1936, when the Aga Khan sold Blenheim to Arthur B.
Hancock Sr, it was clear that British breeders could not afford to
purchase a top class stallion on the open market. This was because
the bloodstock market had not developed sufficiently to justify the
financial risk of speculating on a stallion's ability to pass on the
required attributes. In England horse-racing was still held to be a
sport, and those Americans who found commercialism distasteful
sent their horses to be trained in England. In the United States the
owning and breeding of racehorses were never restricted to the
members of a particular social class, and many welcomed the rising
value of bloodstock as an additional attraction to the sport.

Arthur B. Hancock was one of the first international stallion
entrepreneurs. He started buying proven English racehorses, with a

view to standing them at his Virginia stud farm, during the First World War. In the early 1920s his wife inherited the Claiborne Farm, near Paris, Kentucky, and he moved his operation there. In 1925 he formed the first stallion syndicate, to buy the French horse Sir Gallahad III for $125,000. Sir Gallahad III had been a good but not outstanding racehorse. He won the Lincoln handicap and beat Épinard in a match, but he was receiving eleven pounds. Hancock's rationale was the same as that of anyone who invests in stallions today. If he stood Sir Gallahad at Claiborne he could be certain to persuade people to send him mares for at least four years. After four years the first of his progeny would have had time to prove themselves on the racecourse: if they were successful the gamble would have paid off handsomely, but even if they were not he would already have covered much of his costs. A stallion traditionally covers about forty mares a year, so in the four years before a stallion's merit as a progenitor is known he will cover around 160 mares. This meant that as long as Hancock could persuade people to pay $700 or $800 to have a mare covered by Sir Gallahad, he could recoup much of the original investment – even if the horse's offspring turned out to be predominantly slow.

Hancock could not afford the initial capital outlay himself, so he persuaded some of the leading American breeders of the day to join him in the enterprise, including Marshall Field and William Woodward, who were patrons of Cecil Boyd Rochfort's stable. This spreading of the costs was both an insurance against possible disaster – the horse could have been killed in transit, or infertile – and an advertisement; with such men among the syndicate Hancock could be sure the horse would be sent some of the best American mares, giving him every opportunity to succeed. The novelty value of a European stallion in the United States has since disappeared; so an entrepreneur today would have to be selective in his choice of stallion and then go to great lengths to advertise his potential brilliance, in order to be sure of a full book of mares for the initial four years. Otherwise the rationale would be the same.

As it turned out, Sir Gallahad was a brilliant success. His first crop included Gallant Fox, who won the American Triple Crown for William Woodward, and for the remainder of his life he was fully booked. He was the champion American stallion four times, and amongst the leading twenty on fifteen occasions. Sir Gallahad established Claiborne as America's leading stud farm, a position consolidated by Hancock's next purchase, the Aga Khan's Derby winner Blenheim. Blenheim proved to be a bargain, even at £45,000, as his first American crop included the Tripe Crown winner Whirlaway and he was among the leading twenty stallions on twelve occasions.

Hancock's son, Arthur R. 'Bull' Hancock Jr, took over the running of Claiborne in 1949. He made the farm's most successful purchase yet when he bought Nasrullah from Joseph McGrath in 1950. McGrath had bought Nasrullah for 19,000 guineas in 1945, and he passed him on to the Claiborne syndicate for $37,000. The horse was an immediate success; his son Nashua was the champion American three-year-old in 1955 (he was also the first horse to be syndicated for more than $1 million). Nasrullah was four times champion stallion in the United States, and his offspring included Never Bend, the sire of Mill Reef. When 'Bull' Hancock died in 1972, Claiborne was an enormous commercial enterprise standing many stallions, including the Derby winners Sir Ivor and Nijinsky.

Although there were no equivalents in England of the large Kentucky stud farms, there were some who realized the trend towards commercialism was inevitable. Men like Martin Benson and David Robinson provoked an inordinate amount of ill feeling, for those who ran racing still considered it to be a sport and did not like to be publicly contradicted. Martin Benson was a successful bookmaker and one of the first Englishmen to attempt to make money by investing in stallions. He bought Windsor Lad midway through his three-year-old career, and the colt won the 1934 St Leger in his colours. Benson kept Windsor Lad in training the following season and won four races with him, but decided against taking on the French champion, Brantôme, in the Ascot Gold Cup. This decision was attacked fiercely in the sporting press, and Lord Hamilton of Dalzell, His Majesty's Ascot Representative, wrote to him personally to demonstrate his disapproval. Benson replied, with a degree of honesty that would be considered naïve today: 'My main business is to see he does not get beaten before he retires to stud.' Unfortunately for Benson, Windsor Lad contracted severe sinus problems in 1938 and had to be put down in 1942.

Benson was more successful with his next purchase, the Italian-bred Nearco, whom he bought for £60,000 in 1938. Nearco was a brilliant stallion, figuring among the ten leading sires in Britain for fifteen consecutive seasons; during his last ten seasons at stud, nominations to him often changed hands for more than £2,000. Around half all the top class horses in the world today are descended from Nearco.

David Robinson was the first Englishman to buy large numbers of racehorses for the specific purpose of making money. His father owned a bicycle shop in Cambridge, and his early experiences of racing were gained in the Silver Ring at Newmarket. He amassed a personal fortune through pioneering radio and television rentals and, in 1946, he bought his first racehorse. His first trainer, Ryan Jarvis, remembers that even then he was convinced it would be possible for an outsider like himself, who knew nothing of racing and breeding, to go to sales, learn, and then buy his way to success. For a time his horses were trained by Geoffrey Brooke, with some success, for he won the 1955 Two Thousand Guineas with Our Babu, but it was not until 1968 that he tried to test his theory to the full.

Robinson's idea was that as long as he had one or two horses every year good enough to be sold as stallions, they would pay for the expenses incurred by the others. He bought the Carlburg and Clarehaven stables in Newmarket and installed Paul Davey and Michael Jarvis as his trainers. The team he took on to buy yearlings for him became known as the 'Robinson rangers'; they included the Earl of Harrington and the retired trainer Jack Colling. He originally asked Lord Harrington to buy him thirty classic colts a year, but when he discovered that this number did not come on the market in Britain, he decided to buy one or two potential Derby horses a year and to divide the remainder between Guineas horses and two-year-olds. The number of horses he had in training rose from 98 in 1969 to 157 by 1973, all of whom had been bought for an average of 10,000 guineas – which at the time was considered to be expensive, if not the very top of the market.

Every season from 1968 to 1975, Robinson was the leading owner in terms of individual winners and races won. For five consecutive seasons he had over fifty winners in his colours – green jacket, red sleeves, and a light blue cap – and on three occasions he had more than 100 winners. The 115 winners he had in 1973 are still the most any owner has had in a single season in Great Britain. Perhaps more importantly for him, he also made racing pay, returning an annual profit of between 20 and 25 per cent on his outlay.

Robinson has never been a gregarious man and, although he went racing frequently, he disliked going to collect his prizes and did not attempt to make any racecourse friends. Those who worked with him, most of whom were fond of him, sometimes wondered why he bothered, for he never appeared to be excited or pleased by his successes. The only time he showed any emotion publicly was when his superlative two-year-old, My Swallow, won the Prix de la Salamandre at Longchamp: he produced a tear, confirming the Duke of Devonshire's dictum that victory brings the tears in racing, not defeat. My Swallow was undefeated as a two-year-old, winning seven races including the four most important French races for two-year-olds.

Taking the utmost interest in all his horses, Robinson organized their careers himself. He had a large board in his office with the names of all his two-year-olds written on red pins, for top class, at the beginning of every season. If a horse showed signs of not being top class, his pin was changed for a blue one; finally, for those who were not good, green was the colour. He also had a pin-board marking racecourses as red, blue, and green, and a similar one for jockeys. Only a green jockey could ride green horses on green racecourses – if one of his trainers put a green horse on a red racecourse with a blue jockey he would get the sack.

The racing establishment, with whom he never saw eye to eye, thought Robinson was lowering the tone of racing by openly trying to make money out of it. He considered racing's power structure to be arcane and those who ran it to be incompetent. At the end of the 1977 flat season Robinson sold all his horses and his stables. He had proved his point over ten years, but had lost interest. He had become reclusive, and failed to appear when the Queen opened the new Robinson College he had given to Cambridge University; likewise, although he bought Lord Clark's Turner for £7.5 million, he did so through an agent.

The decline in the international competitiveness of British breeding was such that by the middle 1960s there were only two sources of racehorses of international repute in Britain. The first was the few British owners who still retained a number of high class broodmares; the second was the foreign millionaires who chose to race their horses in England, many of them because they enjoyed the very aspects of British racing that contributed to its decline.

Foremost among the British owner-breeders were Major Lionel Holiday and Jim Joel. Major Holiday bred many good horses, the best being Hetherset – who won the 1962 St Leger and may well have been unlucky not to win the Derby, in which he was brought down – and Vaguely Noble, whom his son sold after his death. Vaguely Noble was sold as a two-year-old at the 1967 December Sales at Newmarket. He had already shown himself to be among the best of his generation and, despite the fact he was not entered in any of the classic races, he fetched the new world record public auction price of 136,000 guineas. The gamble taken by Dr R. Franklyn, an American plastic surgeon, and Nelson Bunker Hunt, who acquired a half-share in the horse soon afterwards, paid off: Vaguely Noble won the 1968 Prix de l'Arc de Triomphe in the style of a true champion, beating the Derby winner Sir Ivor by three lengths. Vaguely Noble is now one of the forty-five stallions standing at the Gainesway Farm in Kentucky.

If you judge how difficult a man is by the number of trainers he gets through, then Major Holiday was a very difficult man indeed. He used to say his trainers came to him on bicycles and left in Bentleys, but they would not all have agreed. There is a story that while one of them was moving into Major Holiday's Lagrange stables in Newmarket, he asked a man who was helping with the furniture whether he considered one room to be too damp for a particularly fine table. He was told not to worry, as the furniture would not be there long enough to get damp, which it was not. Major Holiday was not elected to the Jockey Club until he was over eighty, a few years before his death.

Jim Joel is, by contrast, one of the most popular people in racing today. The only son of Jack Joel, he served in a cavalry regiment during the First World War and is a knowledgeable horseman. He inherited the Childwick Bury Stud in 1940 and immediately set about re-establishing it as one of Britain's leading studs. He won his first classic race with Picture Play in 1944 and had to wait until 1967 for his next, but Royal Palace, who won the Two Thousand Guineas and the Derby, was one of the best English-bred horses of the post-war era.

Joel has won almost every major race in the country with horses that he bred himself. Fairy Footsteps and Light Cavalry, who won the One Thousand Guineas and St Leger respectively, were the best in recent years. He is a member of the Jockey Club, but the only administrative posts he has held are a stewardship at Alexandra Park and membership of the finance committee. He is liked not on account of his brilliance or originality but because he is knowledgeable and charming. Joel still attends almost every Newmarket meeting and can be seen in the paddock, a small, neat man in blue pinstripes, towered over by his trainer, Henry Cecil.

There are few private breeders with sufficient resources to compete at the highest level today. As the best of every American generation are imported to race in Europe, the top races are now more difficult to win than ever before. If there are few breeders who can afford to send mares to be covered in Kentucky, there are not many more able to pay £100,000 for the services of Mill Reef, or the other proven classic stallions standing in Britain. Yet there is still a large element of chance in the breeding of the thoroughbred, and occasionally an unfashionable stallion or broodmare will produce a champion. The chances of this happening were greater before the influx of American-bred horses. Among those who succeeded in doing so were Arthur Budgett, who bred two Derby winners from his mare Windmill Girl, for whom he had paid only 1,000 guineas, and Mr and Mrs John Hislop, who bred Brigadier Gerard.

Brigadier Gerard won seventeen of his eighteen races, over distances ranging from five furlongs to a mile and a half and spread over three seasons. On all but the first three occasions on which he ran he took on the very best company; he twice looked likely to be beaten when running on soft ground, but both times his determination enabled him to win by a narrow margin. When he was beaten at York it took a performance from the 1972 Derby winner, Roberto, that was considerably in advance of anything else he achieved. On the only occasion he met his contemporary Mill Reef, he beat him by three lengths in the 1971 Two Thousand Guineas – although this is not a completely fair reflection of their relative merits, as Mill Reef was better over a longer trip.

The achievements of Brigadier Gerard dominate the East Woodhay Stud where he was reared. A magnificent bronze of him by Professor John Skeaping stands in the garden to be admired by every visitor. The likeness is so real that, as John Hislop says, it would not be a surprise if he stepped off his pedestal. He is a particularly fine-looking horse; to his breeders' delight a French expert who visited him soon after he had taken up his duties as a stallion declared that he was the perfect specimen of the racehorse. As a stallion he has been disappointing, and although it was unfortunate for his future prospects that two of his most promising progeny, Leonardo da Vinci and Admiral's Launch, suffered setbacks from which they never recovered. At the time of writing he has a promising filly in Louis Freedman's Ever Genial.

The numerous successes of American-bred horses in Europe's top races during the late 1960s and early 1970s finally convinced the British racing fraternity of the superiority of the United States breeding industry. These horses were sent to race in Europe partly because victory in the Derby and the other English classic races still conferred a unique prestige upon any animal, but also because a few rich Americans enjoyed the diversity and atmosphere of British racing.

Paul Mellon is one such man. He acquired his love of English racing and its sporting art whilst he was an undergraduate at Cambridge in the 1920s. Encouraged by a fellow American to try hunting, he became something of an addict. He has often hunted with the Middleton and is remembered by some Yorkshire farmers as 'Water Mellon', in memory of an outing that ended up in a cold stream. Mellon is the sort of cultured American who is unashamedly romantic and sentimental about England. At Rokeby, his home in Virginia, he has an outstanding collection of sporting art; for though he has given many of his paintings to institutions, including the Tate Gallery, he retains those he most esteems. Also at Rokeby are his stud and private racing stables. These have produced many American champions, like Key to the Mint and Run the Gantlet, as well as the great Mill Reef.

Mill Reef was one of the most popular horses in England after his racing career and his recovery from an injury that should have been fatal. He won the Derby, the 'Arc', and ten other races, only ever being defeated by My Swallow and Brigadier Gerard. Almost as an act of charity, Mellon arranged for Mill Reef to stand at the National Stud in Newmarket. He has already exerted a considerable influence on British bloodstock, and his son Shirley Heights is the most promising young stallion in Europe today.

Charles Englehard was an American millionaire who took up racing on an even larger scale. He was the son of a German Jewish immigrant to the United States who made his fortune through building up a vast industrial empire originally founded upon the extraction of platinum. This enabled him to indulge in his passion for Coca Cola; he carried a crate of it with him wherever he went.

Englehard first owned racehorses in South Africa, and his victories there made him something of a celebrity. Encouraged, he began to buy horses to race in Europe. When he died in 1971, he owned some 300 horses, who were trained in the United States, England, Ireland, France, and South Africa. Thanks to his Triple Crown winner Nijinsky, he was known and fêted by racing people throughout the world.

Before looking at the dramatic changes of the last ten years, it is worth summarizing the position of British racing and breeding before the advent of the international horse entrepreneurs and the Arabs. It was clear that the overall standard of racing and breeding was higher in the United States than in Europe. In France the appreciation of this fact was accompanied by dramatic and perhaps futile gestures, which included attempts to implement a ban on the importation of American bloodstock. It was soon realized that this would have only guaranteed the decline of French racing. In England there was little response at all, the general attitude being that those trainers who relied upon American-bred horses were unsporting to capitalize on such an unfair advantage. The defeat of an American-bred horse was an event worthy of celebration, and the more an animal had cost at Keeneland, the louder were the cheers. Many of those who were active participants in English racing are still unaware that this was a time when the best racehorses did not compete in Great Britain.

The few world-class racehorses who did compete in Britain were owned by rich foreigners, attracted by the atmosphere and diversity of English racing, and by its traditional prestige. British race-goers have the reputation of being more knowledgeable and more interested in racehorses for their own sake, rather than purely as something to gamble on, than their counterparts anywhere else in the world. Nicholas Robinson, the publisher of *Pacemaker International*, remembers with horror a trip to see Forego, one of the great American horses of the 1970s, run in the United States. By the time Forego made his entrance, half the crowd had left because they had run out of money, having wasted it on the six or seven preceding races. These were all run over the same distance and contested by indistinguishably moderate horses.

Despite this support, the majority of the best horses to race in Europe were exported, or re-exported, to the United States, at the end of their racing careers. There were breeders in England with the equine resources to produce high class horses, but many of them relied upon a few broodmares or upon a particular family. It is rare for an equine family to produce horses of the highest class for more than three consecutive generations, and few English breeders could afford to buy top class racemares or broodmares on the open market. Indeed, one of the reasons for the export of so many stallions was that there were not enough top class broodmares in England to fill the books of more than a handful of them.

Some European racing men understood the need to invest in American blood, notably Alec Head and Captain Rogers of the Airlie Stud, who organized the syndicate who bought Habitat from Charles Englehard in 1969. Few Europeans, however, possessed the time, the energy, or above all the money to go to the United States to buy horses.

The economic recession of the early 1970s had an adverse effect on the British bloodstock market, which led to a further deterioration of the financial position of most British breeders. It has since been proved that the very top of the international bloodstock market is largely unaffected by economic fluctuations, but at the time the British industry played only a small role in such transactions. In 1975 there was a real possibility England would soon become a minor racing nation. This has not happened – indeed, the best racehorses in the world now compete in Great Britain; and if many of them are still bred in the United States, there is good reason to suppose this will not always be the case. To understand this complete transformation we must to look at the racing operations of Robert Sangster, the Maktoum family of Dubai, and Prince Khaled Abdulla.

9

International Entrepreneurs

Robert Sangster was not involved with horses at all until the 1960s, when he bought some racehorses, which he sent to be trained by Eric Cousins, near his home in Cheshire. His father, Vernon Sangster, founded the football pools company that still bears his name. The first horse to run in the Derby wearing the Sangster racing colours – emerald green, royal blue sleeves, and white cap with green spots – was Hang On, who started at 150 to 1 in Royal Palace's Derby and lived up to the bookmakers' expectations by finishing well down the field.

Sangster was not conspicuously successful as an owner until he began his partnership with Vincent O'Brien for although he had some fifty horses with Cousins, his winners were comparatively few. In 1968 he founded the Swettenham Stud with the idea of breeding foals to sell. One of the first good horses to be bred there was Dibidale, whom Nicholas Robinson bought as a foal in 1972. She was unlucky not to win the Oaks, as her saddle slipped two furlongs out; she finished in third place with it hanging under her belly and with Carson riding bareback. She was later disqualified as the cloth carrying weight fell out when the saddle went.

In 1975 Sangster decided to make the owning and breeding of racehorses his business. He was not the first man to appreciate the potential returns from investing in stallions, nor was he the first to conduct his racing on an international basis, but he was the first to try to combine the two. The difference between Sangster and all those who have raced horses on a similar scale is that his primary intention is to make money. The Aga Khan looked to the bloodstock industry to provide him with a return on the money he invested in horses, but his primary aim was to breed and own the best racehorses. The distinction may be a nebulous one, however, and perhaps, had there been the same potential rewards in his day, the Aga Khan would have pursued the same ends.

The distinguishing feature of Sangster's racing enterprise is not its commercialism, nor its internationalism, but its comprehensiveness. Previously the large Kentucky stallion farms, which were at the forefront of the bloodstock industry, would wait until a racehorse had proved himself to be of the highest quality before becoming financially involved – leaving the costs of training and the risks of buying yearlings to others. Some occasionally would race horses they had bred themselves, but only when they were not satisfied with the prices their yearlings were fetching. Sangster knew that the prestige of Europe's top races was still unsurpassed, and that the best bloodstock was reared in the United States. His intention was to buy the best yearlings on offer in the United States, to race them in Europe, and then to sell them back to American breeders, retaining a few shares and a sizeable profit for himself.

His aim was to gain control of a number of the world's best stallions. The attempt to achieve this by buying the best yearlings and hoping they would develop into the best stallions, rather than buying proven racehorses, meant the potential return was far greater, as were the risks. In 1968 Vincent O'Brien bought Nijinsky as a yearling for $80,000; two years later he was syndicated by the Claiborne Farm for $5,440,000. The members of the syndicate have been receiving a return on their investment ever since, and nominations to Nijinsky have been known to change hands for as much as $750,000. Sangster was attracted not only by this long-term return, but also by the spectacular capital appreciation of the very best racehorses. Nijinsky's value increased by almost seventy times in two years, during which time he also earned over £250,000 in prize money.

The risks involved in buying yearlings are numerous. It is difficult enough to predict which of two proven racehorses will be the superior stallion. When buying potential stallions as yearlings, there is the additional problem of deciding which will develop into superior racehorses. A yearling thoroughbred is a very fragile animal and may well break down, or meet with some other injury that prevents it from fulfilling its potential on the racecourse, long before its fertility and ability as a progenitor become a matter for consideration. To reduce these risks it is possible to employ the best judges to select yearlings and then the best trainers and jockeys to ensure the horse has every advantage during its racing career, yet the risks are still great.

Some idea of the problems can be gained from the fact that, of the ten highest priced yearlings bought in Europe in 1983, who cost 7,640,000 guineas between them, only one managed to win a race as a two-year-old, and none of the ten are considered to be destined for classic honours in 1985. The ten highest priced from the United States, who cost an aggregate of $38,700,000, fared a little better, as four of them won. These included Robert Sangster's Law Society and Sheikh Mohammed's Local Suitor, who proved themselves to be among the best of their generation as two-year-olds.

In order to minimize his risks, Sangster was also forced to follow the philosophy of Martin Benson, and to treat the racing careers of his superior colts as an advertising campaign. There are many possible objectives to be considered when planning a horse's racing career. The various alternatives include winning as many races as possible, winning as much prize money as possible, or planning a successful gambling coup. The rationale of Sangster's investment in bloodstock was that the capital appreciation of a good racehorse was far greater than any other possible return, at least for the most fashionably bred colts. Therefore the racing careers of the best yearlings he buys are planned to maximize their appeal to those who wish to buy shares in stallions. This means that to race a colt after he has established a reputation, or if it is felt he has nothing further to gain in the way of prestige, is an expensive luxury.

When in 1975 Sangster first went to the yearling sales to carry out his new policy he was aware of the enormous risk he was taking. He has said himself: 'The only way to succeed in racing and breeding is to go about it professionally and on a big scale. If I had got it wrong I would have been bankrupt in the very first year.' The success of the operation depended upon selecting the right yearlings, and so he realized he had to buy a considerable number. As the Aga Khan had taken on George Lambton to buy his yearlings for him, so Sangster went into partnership with Vincent O'Brien, who was held in similar regard.

In 1944, when he was only twenty-seven, O'Brien set himself up as a trainer in a yard hired from his half-brother. For some years he was predominantly a National Hunt trainer, winning the Grand

National for three consecutive years, four Cheltenham Gold Cups, and three Champion Hurdles, before turning his attention to flat racing. The first top class flat horse he looked after was the American J. McShain's Ballymoss, who won the St Leger in 1957 and the 'Arc' the following year. Perhaps it was the result of his friendship with J. McShain, or his visit to the United States to run Ballymoss in the Washington International in 1959 – whatever the reason, his yard at Ballydoyle, Cashel, Tipperary, was soon full of American-owned and often -bred horses. He bought Raymond Guest's first Derby winner, Larkspur, at the Ballsbridge Sales in Ireland, but he was a regular visitor to the North American yearling sales and bought many of his patrons' horses there. He is now as well known as a judge of young horses as he is as a trainer. Vincent O'Brien's Ballydoyle stables and gallops are said to be the best in Europe, and the preparation of his horses to be the most meticulous. He trains fewer than fifty horses and is entrusted with only the most expensive colts and a few fillies. He was the obvious man for Sangster to go to; not only was his record as a trainer incomparable, but many of his triumphs had been with American-bred horses and he probably had more contacts in the American breeding industry than any other European. To help O'Brien with the selection of yearlings and the breeding side of the operation, Sangster engaged John Magnier, now the manager of his Irish stallion farms. The third member of what Sangster has flippantly called his trinity is the stallion Northern Dancer.

Northern Dancer was bred by the Canadian E. P. Taylor, the dominant breeder in Canada since the 1940s. In the early 1950s, with a view to progressing to international success, he started to buy the best blood available in Britain and the United States. He attended the 1952 December Sales at Newmarket and asked George Blackwell, then with the British Bloodstock Agency, which was the best mare in the sale. He replied that it was a Hyperion mare called Lady Angela, who was in foal to Nearco. Taylor bought the mare, on the condition that she would be covered again by Nearco the following year. Nearco's owner, Martin Benson, agreed because he wanted some money in the United States in order to avoid the exchange controls then in operation in England. The result of this second mating was Nearctic, who won twenty races in Canada. When he was retired to stud in 1960, the last mare he covered during his first season was Natalma, whom Taylor had bought in the United States. The result of this mating was Northern Dancer. Northern Dancer was sent to the sales as a yearling, but since no one wanted to pay the required $25,000 for such a small colt, he was retained by his breeder.

Northern Dancer was the champion two-year-old colt in Canada in 1963, and the following year he was sent to race in the United States. He won both the leading races for three-year-olds in Florida, before being sent north to win the first two legs of the American Triple Crown, the Kentucky Derby and the Preakness Stakes. He won the Kentucky Derby in a new record time of two minutes dead for the mile and a quarter – which has been bettered since only by Secretariat. Surprisingly he was beaten in the last leg of the Triple Crown, the mile-and-a-half Belmont Stakes, some said because he did not stay, while others thought his jockey threw the race away through over-confidence. Then Northern Dancer returned to Canada to win his country's premier race, the Queen's Plate, in front of an enthusiastic crowd, for his American exploits had made him a national hero. He was syndicated for $2,400,000 and took up his stallion duties. In 1967 a mare of Taylor's called Flaming Page, who had been a Canadian champion herself, produced a Northern Dancer colt which Vincent O'Brien bought, on behalf of Charles Englehard, at the Woodbine Sales in Toronto. The colt was named Nijinsky and carried his sire's fame to Europe with his exploits there in 1970.

In 1975 Northern Dancer was a stallion of repute, but, largely as a result of the European successes of his sons who have been raced by Sangster and O'Brien, he is now on a pedestal entirely of his own. In 1970 he became one of the few foreign-based stallions to head the British sires' list; and although he has never left the North American continent he was the leading stallion in Britain in 1977, 1983, and 1984. At least fifteen of Northern Dancer's sons are now established as major stallions in their own right.

Following the commercial policy that it would be foolish to rely upon one man, or one stable, Sangster also sent horses to Barry Hills, Captain Ryan Price, Jeremy Hindley, and Dermot Weld. He maintained the relationship Vincent O'Brien had had previously with Lester Piggott, except that Piggott was now expected to ride his horses in Ireland as well as on their trips abroad. In 1977, the year in which the first generation of Sangster horses were three-year-olds, he was the leading owner in Britain, and his horses won over £600,000 in first-place prize money in Europe. Among the races he won were the Irish One Thousand Guineas, the Derby, the Irish Derby, the 'King George', and the 'Arc', as well as the King's Stand Stakes at Royal Ascot, one of the top spring races, and some of the top two-year-old races, including the Dewhurst Stakes and the Cheveley Park Stakes. More important, in River Dane, Snookera, Lady Capulet, and Durtal, Sangster had four valuable broodmares, the first two of whom he had bred himself, and in The Minstrel and Alleged he had two champions of international repute, whom breeders from all over the world wanted to buy.

The Minstrel is by Northern Dancer and was bred by E. P. Taylor. Sangster had bought him at the Keeneland Sales in Kentucky for $200,000. In August 1977, two years later, Taylor bought back a large share in the horse for $4,100,000; the deal gave The Minstrel a nominal value of $9 million, and the horse's value had appreciated by 4,500 per cent.

Alleged was bought, with two American partners, for $175,000 as a two-year-old in 1976. Sangster bought out one of his partners shortly before the 1977 St Leger, in which Alleged was beaten for the only time in his life. The horse went on to win two Prix de l'Arc de Triomphe and prove himself to have been one of the all-time greats. Sangster had proved that it could work, and that true and proven champions, like The Minstrel and Alleged, were sufficiently valuable to pay for a number of equally well bred but disappointing horses.

Since 1977 Sangster's bloodstock interests have continued to expand and diversify. The most important of these developments is that he has become one of the world's largest breeders. In 1984 he owned an interest in thirty-four stud farms in Europe, Australia, the United States, South Africa, and Venezuela, and he owned 278 broodmares. At the beginning of 1984 seventy-six of the colts he had raced were standing as stallions, and he owned shares in numerous others. Originally his superior colts were syndicated at the end of their racing careers and then returned to the United States, to stand at one of the Kentucky stud farms. His stallions now stand at stud farms throughout the world, and his Coolmore, Castle Hyde, and Associated Stud Farm in Ireland is the largest stallion farm in

Europe, with twenty-one resident there at the beginning of the 1985 covering season. These are mainly horses in whom he has had an interest since their yearling days, but among the purchases of proven horses are Gorytus and Hello Gorgeous.

Sangster has also acquired two racing magazines, *Pacemaker* and *Stud and Stable*, and amalgamated them to produce *Pacemaker International*, a trade magazine that thrives upon American breeding advertisements. It is also rumoured that he owns some of *Timeform*. He has also played a part in the buying and refurbishing of Phoenix Park racecourse near Dublin, and started some spectacular sponsorship, making the Swettenham Stud Sussex Stakes the most valuable race run over a mile in Europe, and sharing with Stavros Niarchos the sponsorship of the Phoenix Champion Stakes. Over the last few years he has also changed his personnel. His major partners are now Daniel Schwartz and Stavros Niarchos, although Vincent O'Brien probably owns as much as fifteen per cent of the horses he trains. Sangster came to an agreement to share some of the most expensive of his American yearlings with Niarchos when they both realized the futility of bidding against each other for the sole benefit of some American breeder. The majority of the horses who race in the Sangster colours are, in fact, owned by a partnership.

In 1980 Sangster had a falling-out with Lester Piggott and since 1981 he has retained Pat Eddery to ride the horses O'Brien trains. Like some of the others Piggott has worked for, Sangster was given cause to wonder by Piggott's individualistic approach.

Sangster was instrumental in persuading the American jockey Steve Cauthen to come to England. Now that Cauthen has left Barry Hills to work for Henry Cecil, he has persuaded the leading Australian jockey Brent Thompson to come and ride for him in England. He has also bought the Manton training stables and a 10,000-acre estate in Wiltshire, where Michael Dickinson will train some of the horses he breeds himself from 1986.

The size of Sangster's racing and breeding concerns is now such that there is hardly an aspect of the industry in which he is not concerned. At the beginning of the 1984 season he had 421 horses in training, 221 of which were in Europe, 136 in Australia, and 64 elsewhere in the world. Of this last category the majority were in the United States, though he also had horses in New Zealand, South Africa, and Venezuela. He is now extensively engaged in the

Martin Benson (*W.W. Rouch*)

Charlie Elliott (*W.W. Rouch*)

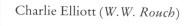

(*Left*) Mr and Mrs John Hislop's Brigadier Gerard with Joe Mercer up, after winning the 1972 King George VI and Queen Elizabeth II Stakes at Ascot (*W.W. Rouch*)

(*Left, below*) Paul Mellon with his trainer Ian Balding (*Gerry Cranham*)

(*Below*) Noel Murless, Alec Head, and Jim Joel on Derby day, 1977 (*Gerry Cranham*)

(*Above*) The 6th Earl of Rosebery (*W.W. Rouch*)

(*Left*) The Queen and Lord Porchester, her racing manager, at Newbury (*Rex Features Ltd*)

(*Right*) The Maktoums and friend in the winners enclosure, Royal Ascot, 1985 (*Gerry Cranham*)

(*Left, below*) Sheikh Mohammed leading in Oh So Sharp and Steve Cauthen after the 1985 Oaks (*Gerry Cranham*)

(*Right, below*) Prince Khaled Abdulla with Guy Harwood (*Gerry Cranham*)

Lester Piggott (*Express Newspapers*)

Robert Sangster and Lester Piggott
(*Gerry Cranham*)

Robert Sangster with Vincent
O'Brien, Derby day, 1978
(*Gerry Cranham*)

Lord Howard de Walden with Slip Anchor and Steve Cauthen after the 1985 Derby (*Gerry Cranham*)

exchange of foals, yearlings, broodmares, and stallions on five continents.

From being just another rich man, Sangster has become an international figure, particularly fêted in Australia, and his private life has become of interest to the readers of the popular press. Twice married, he has moved to the Isle of Man, although his Swettenham Stud is still a British-based company. He now leads the sort of hetic life only the very rich can afford, being continually on the move, chasing the bloodstock circus from Keeneland in July, to Newmarket, to Ireland, and back to Kentucky. He also follows the main events in the racing calendar and spends some months in Australia every winter. His visits to London are now rare, and timed to coincide with only very important events, like Frank Sinatra concerts.

To watch Sangster on the racecourse or at the sales is to realize that most of the time he enjoys his business. He loves to gamble and will bet on races like the Two Thousand Guineas even when any winnings are likely to be insignificant compared with the capital appreciation of his horse, should it win. He also enjoys the racecourse gossip and atmosphere and the friendship of such racecourse figures as Charles Benson of the *Daily Express*. He has not become pompous and is polite to those who approach him – although, now that he has become highly knowledgeable about horseracing, his patience with those who are not has diminished. In many ways he is a shy man, preferring the company of those with whom he is familiar. On the day of a big race, or a big sale, the excitement and tension are obvious; he cannot keep still and cannot stop having whispered conferences with confederates. He is not one for exuberant celebrations, preferring to retire to another quiet corner, only allowing a slight relaxation of his habitually worried look.

Sangster is sensitive to what is written about him and the way his horses are run. At times he appears to be almost jealous when others are praised. He goes to considerable lengths to point out that those of his horses who are robust have full racing careers and are not rushed off to stud after one good performance. Moreover, he is keen to show that he wants to put something back into racing and to provide entertainment.

He is not a flamboyant man; and although he has been known to give lavish parties, his wife and children do the majority of the

Sangster socializing. Outside racing, he is a dedicated backgammon player and has been known to go out after woodcock in Waterford with John Magnier and Vincent O'Brien, but they have usually had far too good a lunch to hit anything. Few people on the racecourse bear him any personal grudge.

Officially, Sangster's horse-breeding and racing activities are said to have made an enormous contribution to the Vernons Organisation's total net profits in recent years. Yet there have been persistent rumours, dampened by the appearance of El Gran Señor and Sadler's Wells, that this is not, in fact, the case. Some of the rumours are the result of nothing more than envy, or a dislike of the effect he has had on British racing, whilst he has only to be seen leaving New-market in a hurry in order to catch a commercial flight from Cam-bridge for it to be announced that he is on the road to bankruptcy. Nevertheless, the scale of Sangster's bloodstock empire is now such that he needs major successes every year to pay the running expenses.

It is impossible for an outsider to produce an accurate estimate of Sangster's annual expenditure on his bloodstock enterprises, with their intricate partnerships and international spread of activities. Of his 421 horses in training, almost all are with the best and most expensive trainers. If veterinary fees and the amount spent on enter-ing a horse in races are included, a rough estimate would be that each horse costs £12,000 a year to keep. Although he owns enough shares in stallions not to have to pay stallion fees – he can always swop nominations if he wishes to use someone else's stallion – it probably costs at least £10,000 to rear each of his foals from birth until they are ready to enter a training stable. This figure takes into account the running costs of a stud and the wages of its staff. Sangster's studs now produce around 200 foals annually. By sending his mares to be covered by his own stallions he incurs a large opportunity cost, for stallion fees account for a significant proportion of his income.

Sangster must have a considerable wage bill to pay, besides the wages of those who work in his studs and stables. His jockeys and advisers are among the best in the world; indeed, Pat Eddery is said to be the highest paid British jockey. Other annual expenses are sec-urity, advertising, and insurance. Security is important at both training stables and stud farms; there are those who believe Sangs-ter's champion two-year-old of 1977, Try My Best, was 'got at', and

Shergar's abduction highlighted the need for vigilance. In 1983 £250,000 was spent on security at the Coolmore Stud alone. Coolmore was the first European stud to produce an annual promotional video extolling the virtues of its resident stallions – the advertising of stallions has become a necessity in a competitive market.

The number of horses Sangster owns probably means he only ever insured his stallions. With his unproven horses it would almost certainly have been cheaper to lose one or two than to have insured the lot. Stallion insurance has become more expensive recently – when insurance companies first took on bloodstock insurance they had little idea of the risks involved. The top class stallions to have died prematurely in recent years include the Derby winners Shergar, Troy, and Golden Fleece, as well as such as Pitcairn, Moorestyle, Nebbiolo, and Double Form, all of whom were younger than ten at the time of death. As a result the premiums for insurance against death or infertility in stallions are high: it cost Maktoum Al Maktoum $8 million to insure Shareef Dancer for five years. Since the death of Golden Fleece, and his subsequent disagreement with Lloyds, Sangster no longer insures any of his horses. This must have reduced his running expenses considerably, although at the same time increasing the risks of his operation.

On top of these running expenses comes Sangster's annual investment in new blood. To estimate the amount of money he spends on yearlings is difficult, not only because he purchases at the leading sales throughout the world, but also because his yearlings are bought in the name of either the British Bloodstock Agency or the British Bloodstock Agency (Ireland), and both these organizations buy for other people besides their most important client. Perhaps it is not too fanciful to suppose Sangster spent some £20 million on yearlings in 1983. He announced during Royal Ascot in 1985 that he did not buy a single yearling in 1984, so as the two organizations signed for yearlings that had cost nearly $40 million at the two main summer sales in Kentucky in 1984, it must be presumed they were purchased on behalf of some of the other patrons of Vincent O'Brien's stable. Sangster also spends a large amount on broodmares at public auction and on proven racehorses in private sales.

The income Sangster receives from his enterprise is largely derived from four sources: the prize money earned by his horses; the sale of some of the yearlings he breeds; the syndication of his proven racehorses before they take up duties as stallions; and the fees he receives from breeders who send their mares to be covered by his stallions. The level of prize money in Britain is lower than in any other major racing nation and, even taking into account the horses he has in training elsewhere, Sangster's horses will never win more than about £1 million a year.

At the present his breeding operation is at a formative stage, and, in Europe at least, it is more geared to producing horses he will race himself than to rearing yearlings for sale. So, for the present, the success of Sangster's operations depends upon his annual purchases of yearlings including racehorses of sufficient calibre to be syndicated as stallions. The reason for speculation about his financial position is that not everything has gone right for him since his first glorious season, and many feel he has had trouble selling shares in some of his stallions.

A stallion is traditionally syndicated into forty shares, with each shareholder having the right to send a mare to be covered by the stallion or to sell his nomination to another breeder. Today successful stallions cover more like sixty mares a year, the exact number each covers being the result of an awkward financial decision. The more mares a stallion covers the greater is his owners' income, but the odds against him producing a good horse are reduced. Yet if there is a glut of a stallion's progeny, the average price his offspring fetch as yearlings may fall, which will damage his reputation. No stallion owner wants his protégé to cover a bad mare, for slow offspring are a bad advertisement. This increase in the number of mares a stallion covers does not necessarily call for a greater degree of energy on his part, as the most efficient stallion farms have reduced the average number of coverings required for a pregnancy from two and a half to one and a half.

It may be announced that a horse has been syndicated for a sum giving him a value of $40 million, but unless every one of the shares in the horse has changed hands for $1 million this is only a nominal value. It may be that one or two very rich people have bought a share, but that the original owners are left with the majority of the shares, and the risks, themselves. The number of people willing to pay $1 million for a share in a stallion is small; and unless they are interested, his real value will be considerably less. Many of these syndication announcements are little more than an advertisement.

Similarly it is accepted that nomination fees are as much promotional as anything else. Until a stallion has proved himself a capable and consistent progenitor – something that will take at least six years and three generations of horses who have proved themselves on the racetrack – it will pay a stallion owner to give large concessions to those mares likely to produce fast racehorses or expensive yearlings. For a stallion to remain commercially viable in the long run, he must produce yearlings who fetch large prices, and good winners in his early crops. A stallion depends upon the quality of the broodmares he covers for his success, and no amount of advertising will sustain his reputation unless he produces results, quickly.

In 1984 there were around 700 stallions standing in Britain and Ireland. Only a fraction of these will cover as many as forty mares a year. Thus although it may be announced that a nomination to a young stallion will cost 50,000 guineas, the owner of a good broodmare will be able to obtain one for considerably less.

A good broodmare is one who produces fast racehorses. A mare's temperament and natural ability as a mother play a significant role in the development of any racehorse, but from the point of view of a stallion owner there are three attributes that will encourage him to give concessions to a mare. The mares of most highly priced yearlings were either good racemares themselves, or they have already produced a significant winner, or they are related to either a good winner or a broodmare who has produced a good winner. For a young mare the first is the most important factor: therefore, although an unfashionably bred colt will never be worth a fortune, however good he may be on the racecourse, a good racemare will be worth a lot of money even if her antecedents were previously undistinguished as progenitors. A mare who combines all three attributes will be worth millions of pounds.

A popular method for giving concessions is foal sharing, when the owner of a high class mare pays nothing to have her covered, but in return gives the stallion's owner a share in the offspring. This sort of deal is not limited to young stallions. An English breeder received a letter from a Kentucky stallion farm in 1984 asking him if he wanted to send three of his mares to three of the world's most expensive stallions, for nothing, but a half-share in any foals who resulted.

To return to Robert Sangster and his finances: in estimating the return on his investment in bloodstock, it would be misleading to take the nomination fees of his stallions and the value of their syndications too literally. Of the 'champions' Sangster has raced since 1977, neither Try My Best, Storm Bird, Danzatore, nor Monteverdi trained on after successful two-year-old careers. Although they are all now at stud, they would have been more valuable, and easier to sell shares in, if they had maintained their superiority for two seasons. Try My Best has since had fertility problems, with only a small percentage of the mares he covers conceiving.

Many people, moreover, feel Sangster had difficulty in syndicating Lomond, Caerleon, and Solford, three of his major winners in 1983. Lomond and Solford had only a few top class performances to their names, and although Caerleon was tough and consistent he was no great champion.

The most serious blow Sangster has suffered in recent years was the death of Golden Fleece, the best potential stallion he has raced since Alleged. Although he ran only four times and won an undistinguished Derby, Golden Fleece showed he possessed a fine turn of foot and beat the only top class horse he ever met – his owner's colt Assert – twice very easily. He had only about thirty foals before his death from cancer. The loss of income from fees, coupled with insurance problems, must have constituted a serious setback.

Sangster has also had considerable success, notably with Assert, who won both the French and Irish Derbys before joining his grandsire, Northern Dancer, at E. P. Taylor's Maryland farm. The 1984 season was a marvellous one for Sangster, with his Northern Dancer colts El Gran Señor and Sadler's Wells both proving themselves to be very good, although the former's mouth must have reduced his value as a stallion. (El Gran Señor has a parrot mouth, which means his lower jaw extends beyond his upper jaw, making it difficult for him to eat from the ground.)

Sangster's original approach to horse-racing and breeding, and the enormous funds he injected into the industry, had an immediate effect on the bloodstock world. His initial investments coincided with a shift in governmental policy towards racing in Ireland and the United States. In both countries various measures were passed specifically intended to encourage the bloodstock industry. The slow progression of the industry towards an unashamedly commercial stance was already accelerating in the early 1970s. Sangster's investments accentuated this progression and gave encouragment to others who hoped to make money out of bloodstock. The real value of bloodstock of all ages began to rise, together with an appreciation in the relative value of yearlings.

In the early years the market for the most fashionably bred yearlings – chiefly but not exclusively consisting of the offspring of Northern Dancer – became almost monopsonistic. When Stavros Niarchos managed to outbid Sangster for the Northern Dancer colt later named Nureyev (first past the post in the 1980 Two Thousand Guineas, only to be disqualified), they swiftly decided to form a partnership to avoid a repetition. Yet from the late 1970s certain Arabs began to show an interest in buying the best bloodstock. It was to Known Fact, a horse owned by Prince Khaled Abdulla, that the 1980 Two Thousand Guineas was awarded, and in 1979 the Maktoum brothers of Dubai showed they were prepared to pay extravagant prices for yearlings by giving 625,000 guineas for a yearling by Lyphard at the Newmarket Sales. Since 1980 Robert Sangster has had to compete for the best lots at sale rings throughout the world with Prince Khaled Abdulla and the Maktoums, and these three racing concerns have changed the pattern of racing internationally.

Whatever the reasons may be for the Maktoum brothers' investment in bloodstock, their intention has never been to make money. Sheikh Mohammed Bin Rashid Al Maktoum and his brothers Hamdan Al Maktoum and Maktoum Al Maktoum are very, very rich. They are all reputed to have a weekly income of at least $1 million; so for them all decisions are personal and never commercial. Those who say Maktoum Al Maktoum retired his Irish Derby winner, Shareef Dancer, because he feared the horse's commercial value would drop if he were beaten subsequently are mistaken. He retired the horse for entirely personal reasons, a major influence on the decision being his horror of seeing a horse he worshipped beaten and then maligned in the sporting press. The colt's trainer, Michael Stoute, was keen to run him in the 1983 Benson & Hedges Gold Cup, yet he was withdrawn on the morning of the race, on account of the heavy overnight rain. Most of those connected with Shareef Dancer were sure he would win – rain or no rain – but his owner was not prepared to take the risk, and the horse was withdrawn and retired to stud: the winner of three of his five races.

The Maktoums probably chose to race in England for much the

same reasons as the numerous American and Indian millionaires who have supported English racing in the past. They were attracted by the traditional veneer of English racing, its historical standing, and the atmosphere of its racecourses. Their interest is in horses and initially their intention was to buy and race the best, whilst in recent years they have become more interested in the breeding side. The Maktoums are different from the numerous other millionaires who have indulged in racing only in the degree of their wealth and the scale of their racing activities. In 1984 they had 350 horses in training, with almost every major trainer in the British Isles looking after a few of them. They have also sent many valuable horses to trainers not considered to be in the first rank of their profession.

Their outlay on yearlings has been on an unprecedented scale, and they have dominated the major sales in Europe and the United States during recent years. In 1982 they spent £27 million on yearlings; in 1983 the figure had reached £50 million; and in 1984 they spent even more. At the Keeneland July Sales (the premier yearling sale in the United States) they spent more than $52 million. In 1984 they bought thirteen of the thirty lots that made more than $1 million at Keeneland, a third of the top eighteen lots at the Tattersall's High-flyer Sales (England's premier yearling sales, in Newmarket), and half the top sixteen lots at Goffs Invitation Sale (Ireland's premier yearling sales).

The Maktoums have been equally to the fore at the sales of broodmares, buying such as Prayer 'n' Promises for $3,750,000 and Avum for $3,200,000 at public auctions. They have also bought numerous proven racemares in private sales, including the Queen's Height of Fashion and the English classic winners Scintillate, Ma Biche, and Pebbles. They now own many studs in England and Ireland including Dalham Hall, Aston Upthorpe, Gainsborough, Derrinstown, and Woodpark. Their operations are still expanding, as Sheikh Mohammed eventually intends to race over 100 of each generation himself.

Until 1985 the return the brothers received from such a bewildering outpouring of petrodollars was pathetic. The Maktoums and their advisors have not begun to emulate the percentages achieved by Robert Sangster and Prince Khaled Abdulla. Of all the horses they raced until the end of the 1984 season only five won a Group One race in the British Isles or France – Group One races are the top

fifty run annually in Europe. They won six Group One races between them, including five classic wins. By way of comparison, since
1980 Sangster has raced twelve Group One winners, who won
twenty-one Group One races between them, including eight classic
wins, and these figures take into account only the horses who ran in
his colours and exclude such classic winners as King's Lake and
L'Émigrant, in whom he owned a share. By the end of 1984 Sangster
had raced a total of twenty-nine Group One winners, who won
forty-four Group One races between them, including fifteen classic
wins.

Of course the Maktoums did not have the advantage of Vincent
O'Brien, and in the early years their lack of experience of hard commercialism led to a certain naïveté of selection. The provincialism of
the racing world meant that it was a few years before all trainers and
bloodstock agents took the Maktoums seriously, and for a time the
less scrupulous saw them merely as a source of easy money. Some of
the horses they bought did not have the conformation and looks to
match their breeding, or even dams of the same quality as their sires.

Today the situation has changed. In 1985 the brothers were able
to dominate the major races with such as Shadeed, Bairn and Al
Bahathri, whom they had bought at public auction, and Sheikh
Mohammed's home-bred filly, Oh So Sharp. Rather than having
too few worthy trainers and advisors they now appear to have an
overabundance of both: they had to charter a large commercial jet to
bring them all from Britain to Keeneland Sales in July 1984. It is the
modern fashion for any large owner to reduce unnecessary costs and
risks of infection by spreading his horses between many different
trainers. However, the example of those who have raced success-
fully on a large scale in the past suggests that it is imperative for the
selection of yearlings and broodmares to be the responsibility of a
handful of men, and for there to be a definite overall policy. The Aga
Khan relied upon George Lambton, Richard Dawson, and Colonel
Vuillier; Marcel Boussac relied upon Marcel Boussac; it would
appear that the Maktoums rely upon an ever-expanding committee.

Sheikh Mohammed, although not the oldest of the brothers, acts
as their spokesman and has the strongest influence over their racing
concerns. He is also the Defence Minister of Dubai, where visitors
to his office are confronted by a fearsome, though stuffed, tiger. His
Dalham Hall Stud, near Newmarket, is the English centre of their

operations and it is there he has built himself an English residence. From Dalham Hall a full list of the brothers' runners, results, and video tapes of races are sent to Dubai when their considerable governmental responsibilities mean they are unable to be in England themselves. Shareef Dancer, the most esteemed of their six stallions, stands at Dalham Hall, and some of the best of their many broodmares board there.

The office at Dalham Hall has more of the air of a London merchant bank than a Newmarket stud. It includes a couple of secretaries, a computer, and a sitting room that would not be incongruous next to any boardroom. The manager of Dalham Hall is the Honourable Robert Acton. Born in Rhodesia, when his family moved to Europe Acton worked as a stud hand on various English and German stud farms before taking up a minor post at the National Stud in Newmarket. As an impoverished stud hand, he sold his two broodmares, one of whom was Hardiemma who produced a selling plater and the Derby winner Shirley Heights within a few years. His appointment as Sheikh Mohammed's stud manager caused some surprise, but as his most evident qualities are honesty and a spontaneous interest in those whom he meets, it must have been a welcome change to deal with him. His excitement after the success of one of Sheikh Mohammed's horses is as striking as it is rare to see someone so involved with their employers' fortunes.

The Maktoums have introduced customs that for a time bewildered the racing world. When Sheikh Maktoum Al Maktoum used to go to the Newmarket July course after racing to watch Shareef Dancer do some work, he would arrive in a convoy of black limousines filled with his fellow countrymen. If asked who they were, he would reply they were his friends and companions; one is an expert falconer, another a fine judge of a camel, a third a skilled swordsman, and all have been with him since childhood. The racing world is not a particularly cosmopolitan one, and only with difficulty were some of the Maktoums' trainers convinced that these gentlemen did not want bacon and eggs for breakfast after watching their horses exercise.

In fact, the Maktoums have displayed a greater consideration for English racing mores than the racing world has shown for Arab traditions. The brothers have been invited out with the Jockey Club shoot, where they impressed everyone with their willingness to help, even when it came to pushing Land-Rovers out of deep mud. Although it is now normal to hear gentlemen exchanging the traditional Arab greetings around the sales ring at Newmarket, many of those who do so are wearing huskies, corduroys, and flat caps.

Prince Khaled Abdulla has a different approach to racing. Although he is similarly wealthy, he has decided to run his bloodstock on the same lines as he would run a business. His intention is simply to breed and race the best horses, but he appreciates the need for patience and planning and has avoided buying yearlings at the very top of the American market. He is an intelligent and sophisticated man who attended Havard University in the United States. He appears to be at ease on British racecourses, bespectacled and favouring brown suits, often accompanied by his racing manager, James Delahooke. The Prince likes to be known in England as Mr Khaled Abdulla, even though he is a senior member of the Saudi Arabian Royal Family, and he displays a similar diffidence in his reluctance to accept publicly the prizes won by his horses.

Khaled Abdulla's first racing manager, Humphrey Cottrill, remembers that their association started when a friend came up to him on Newbury racecourse and told him to come and meet one of the richest men in the world. After a further meeting it was arranged for Cottrill to buy him five yearlings; the following year this was increased to twenty; when it became clear Khaled Abdulla was planning a large, long-term investment in bloodstock, Cottrill stepped down, his post being taken by the youthful James Delahooke. Among the first yearlings Abdulla bought was a colt by In Reality, acquired cheaply at an unfashionable bloodstock sale in Florida. Named Known Fact, the colt proved to be a good two-year-old, winning the 1979 Middle Park Stakes. The following year, besides being awarded the Two Thousand Guineas, he became only the second horse to beat Kris, when winning the Queen Elizabeth II Stakes at Ascot. Humphrey Cottrill could never understand the calm manner in which his employer accepted these victories.

James Delahooke was reared on a stud farm and for a time rode in point-to-points and as an amateur under National Hunt rules. He became a bloodstock agent as the result of a drink with friends at the Bedford Lodge Hotel in Newmarket. When he was taken on by Abdulla, he was in his thirties and already known as an outstanding judge of a young horse, due to the success he had had buying yearlings for the patrons of Guy Harwood's stable. As is the case with all successful dealers, it is impossible to explain Delahooke's talent except by saying he has a good eye. On arrival at a sale he will have a quick look at a number of yearlings and decide which he likes, discarding the rest. He will return to those he liked with someone else and then make a further close examination, with the help of a vet, before making his final selection. He has found that his first impressions are only rarely altered by closer inspection, and provided he has a break every few hours he can look at hundreds of yearlings a day without his judgement being affected.

As racing manager Delahooke's job is to buy Khaled Abdulla's yearlings, to act as a liaison between him and his trainers, and to manage his breeding operation. Abdulla does not necessarily buy at the top of the market; indeed, it is noticeable that few sons or grandsons of Northern Dancer have carried his pink and green colours (he is supposed to have chosen them after admiring some pink and green curtains, in the office of his friend Lord Weinstock). If you are not after such horses, yearlings are comparatively cheap. At the summer sales in Kentucky in 1984, Delahooke purchased sixteen yearlings at an average of $480,000, and he was a prominent buyer at the Highflyer Sales, spending over £2 million on the first and most select day alone.

At the beginning of the 1984 season Abdulla had 135 horses in training. The majority of them were with Jeremy Tree and Guy Harwood, although he also had some with others including Bill Elsey. He asked Elsey to give some rides to a leading Saudi Arabian jockey, which posed considerable problems of communication, as the only Arabic phrasebook on sale in Malton was clearly not written with the idea of helping a trainer give instructions to his jockey.

Khaled Abdulla has been a conspicuously successful owner. In 1984 he was challenging Robert Sangster for the position of leading owner, in terms of prize money won, and Sheikh Mohammed for the honour of winning the largest number of races. Amongst his horses were three of the best three-year-old colts: Rainbow Quest, Alphabatim, and Rousillon. In the years to come he is certain to become a leading breeder, as he now owns the Ferrans Stud in Ireland and Juddemonte Farms in Berkshire; the latter is the best equipped and most modern of stud farms, and the home of Known Fact. He owns eighty broodmares based at Juddemonte, when they are not away being covered by outside stallions, and in 1985 he will race thirty home-bred two-year-olds.

The racing concerns of Robert Sangster, the Maktoum brothers and Khaled Abdulla may have only speeded up developments that would have taken place eventually. However, their intervention has led to sudden changes in the racing world, and to an unexpected revival in the standing of British racing and breeding.

10

Horse-racing Today

The bloodstock industry has been transformed during the last ten years. For confirmation of this one has only to look at the prices horses now fetch at public auction. In 1975 the average price of yearlings at Tattersall's select sale in Newmarket was 7,500 guineas; in 1984 this figure was 95,000 guineas – a rise of nearly 500 per cent, even after inflation has been taken into account. A similar progression has taken place in the United States, with the average price at the Keeneland July Sales rising from $50,000 to $600,000 in the same period.

European and world record prices for foals, yearlings, broodmares, stallion syndications, and stallion nominations are now broken every year. The increased value of broodmares has been especially noticeable. The gap between the value of the highest priced yearlings and the sums stallions are syndicated for has narrowed.

The other notable change of the last ten years is in the international standing of British and Irish racing and breeding. There can be no doubt that the best racehorses are now trained in Britain and Ireland. French stables have won only one race in Britain in the last two years, while numerous horses trained in Britain have won top races in France, the United States, Italy, Germany, and Belgium – and many of those were not among the best of their age group in Britain. Every year the pick of the United States foal crop is exported to Europe, and most of these select yearlings are now trained in Britain or Ireland. Breeding in the British Isles has received a tremendous boost. Not only have many stallions remained in Europe which would once have returned to the United States after their racing careers, but the number of high quality broodmares in Europe has risen enormously as well. Kentucky is still the centre of the world's bloodstock industry, but it is no longer certain this will always be the case.

Those who work in the racing world, and those who follow horse-racing on the racecourse or on television, have benefited from this advance in the relative standing of British racing. Some of the new money in racing has filtered down, and many trainers, jockeys, stable lads, and stud hands now earn their livelihood working for either Sangster or the Arabs. Those who enjoy racing as a spectacle are treated daily to the sight of the best racehorses, ridden by the best jockeys, competing in fairly run races. Yet despite this general aura of well-being there are sections of the racing world that have been adversely affected, and in some ways those who look to racing for entertainment, and the racehorse itself, have suffered.

Firstly, among the adverse effects on the breeding side of racing, the increase in the value of all categories of bloodstock has once again led to the demand for the best racehorses being severely restricted. Initially, as we saw, the growing commercialization of racing allowed a far greater and more varied collection of people the chance of owning a Derby winner or a top class racehorse. As recently as 1975 Dr Carlo Vittadini bought his Derby winner, Grundy, for only 11,000 guineas. Although it is not impossible that a horse from a similar price range will win the Derby again, the chances of this happening have been greatly reduced. Henbit, who won the Derby in 1980, was also a cheap yearling, but he was bought at an unfashionable American sale, and in the last four years the agents of the leading racing concerns have come to dominate even such sales.

There will always be horses who belie their breeding and prove to be superior to their antecedents and relatives. Also, when yearling prices are determined by fashion and whim there will always be young stallions whose offspring are undervalued. An example of the latter was Ballard Rock, the sire of England's champion miler in 1984, Chief Singer. He was a good racehorse, but because his best performances were in Irish handicaps he did not receive the support and publicity he deserved, until he proved himself by siring Chief Singer. The 1984 season gave further evidence of the uncertainties of breeding and of the danger of assuming there is a close connection between the price a yearling fetches and its ability on the racecourse. Of the four Group One races for two-year-olds run in Britain, two were won by horses who had cost less than 20,000 guineas as yearlings.

However, a horse does not have to win a Group One race for its owner to be tempted by offers from one of the leading racing concerns or a commercial breeder. In the spring of 1984 a horse called High Debate rather unexpectedly finished second in a classic trial at Newmarket. Sheikh Mohammed decided to buy him on the strength of this performance and is said to have offered £2 million for the colt. The owner refused to sell, and the horse has still to win a race since. An owner has to be either very rich, very sentimental, or very foolish to refuse such an offer.

The increased value of bloodstock has given the risk of buying a cheap yearling something of the appeal of trying to win the football pools. An unfashionably bred horse may suddenly be worth £500,000, but at the same time it has meant that no owner can afford to ignore the commercial side of racing.

If the demand for the best racehorses is now in danger of being restricted to a few millionaires and professional speculators, then much the same thing is happening on the supply side. The phenomenal prices given at the top of the market obscure the plight of many small breeders who are finding it increasingly difficult to remain solvent. Only three per cent of the annual foal crop are sold at select bloodstock sales, and although there has been a rise in both the aggregate and average prices at lesser sales, they have not been of the same proportion as the rises recorded at the select sales. The small breeder faces the same conundrum as the small owner: if he succeeds in buying a successful broodmare cheaply he will almost certainly have to accept the first extravagant offer he receives, being unable to justify the financial gamble of refusing. The price of a nomination to a successful stallion and the higher standard of racing have reduced a small breeder's chances of producing a good winner; even if he succeeds, he will have to be rich or foolish to keep the broodmare or her successful offspring.

There are still some who can afford to breed their own horses and hope to win classic races. Among those whose colours are well known in Britain are Sir Philip Oppenheimer, E. B. Moller (whose home-bred Teenoso won the 1983 Derby), Louis Freedman (who now owns the Cliveden Stud), Daniel Wildenstein, and, of course, Her Majesty the Queen. There is a famous story that when Princess

Elizabeth was asked, shortly before her coronation, if she was happy with the arrangements, she replied that she had spoken to Captain Boyd Rochfort that morning and Aureole had worked very well. Her colt Aureole finished second in the Derby three days after the coronation. The Queen's long and enthusiastic involvement with racing has added considerably to the sport's popularity as an entertainment. The Royal Procession at Ascot achieves the remarkable feat of emptying the bars, something that even the finest racing never manages to do. The traditionalists would say there are only two real English breeders – where 'real' means those who rear their own horses and never sell them as yearlings: the Queen and Lord Howard de Walden.

Lord Howard de Walden's father was a prominent owner for thirty years. He was also a great patron of the theatre, writing many plays and the librettos for three operas; he is said to have remained in the paddock, sitting under a tree engrossed in one of these, while his horses Zinfandel was winning the 1924 Ascot Gold Cup. Lord Howard himself has been keen on racing for a long time. As a boy he was sent by his father to Newmarket to watch a filly of his called Sunstrie. His father displayed his eccentricity by putting his son and heir in the charge of Bob Sievier for the train journey, though to his son's disappointment Sievier fulfilled his responsibilities admirably. Sunstrie won her race, ridden by a young apprentice called Charlie Elliott, her victory being greeted by such piercing cries from her owner's representative that Sommerville Tattersall and Sir Edward Elgar were moved to tell him to behave and quieten down.

Another of the eighth Baron's eccentricities was, despite owning a large part of the West End of London, to manage to convince himself and his son that the ever-increasing burden of taxation was reducing him, if not exactly to penury, to a state in which he was unable to afford racehorses. The eighth Baron died immediately after the end of the war. When Lord Howard de Walden returned after being demobilized and read the will, his first action was to send Jack Waugh, who had been his father's trainer, to the Doncaster sales with instructions to buy the best filly on offer.

Lord Howard de Walden bought the dam of his most famous broodmare from Sir Victor Sassoon's widow. After Sir Victor's death, Lady Sassoon got into some financial trouble and asked Sir Noel Murless, who had trained and managed her husband's horses, to sell some of her bloodstock. At this time the Sassoon mares were indisputably the best in the country; so when Murless asked Lord Howard if he was interested he did not hesitate to accept, despite the fact that he had to buy a stud in Yorkshire as well as the eight mares he wanted.

The pick of these mares was Soft Angels, who had been the best two-year-old filly of 1965 but had failed to train on. Soft Angels produced only two fillies, the first of whom was a decent winner called Dulcit, who died of grass sickness; the second was Doubly Sure. After showing promise in her first race Doubly Sure failed to achieve anything further on the racecourse, although in the words of her owner she did once manage to come second at Thirsk in the middle of the night. He had planned to sell her, but on Dulcit's death Lord Howard de Walden decided to give Doubly Sure a chance and told his stud groom to send her to something fast. The groom decided to send her to Sharpen Up because he had been a fast two-year-old and was standing down the road at a modest fee.

The result of this mating was Kris, who won fourteen of his sixteen races over three years and distances from five furlongs to a mile. Within five years Sharpen Up was standing for a six-figure fee at Gainesway Farm in Kentucky, alongside the world's best stallions. Doubly Sure has proved to be a remarkable broodmare, for besides Kris she has produced the champion two-year-old Diesis; another full brother, Keen – who has yet to live up to his magnificent looks and the gallops he did in the spring of his three-year-old career, but has shown himself to be a good horse; and Presidium, who is by General Assembly, a beautiful mover and one of the more promising two-year-olds of 1984. Presidium's owner is in the unusual position of wondering where he will eventually go to stud. For with Kris in England, Diesis in the United States, and Keen destined for Australia, Doubly Sure's blood is already spread across the world.

Owning twenty-three mares and three studs in Yorkshire, Newmarket, and near his home in the Hungerford area, Lord Howard de Walden also considers buying shares in stallions to be a good investment. The most remunerative of those he owns is the one in Shirley Heights, which he bought when he happened to be staying with Lord Halifax at the same time as the Queen, at whose Sandringham Stud Shirley Heights now stands. When Ruth, Countess of Halifax asked if he wanted to buy a share he felt it would be disloyal to refuse. Shirley Heights is now the most successful young stallion in Britain and the sire of his Derby winner, Slip Anchor.

Lord Howard de Walden's enthusiasm for racing is unmistakable and at times amusing. When he has an important runner, he and his wife always appear with something apricot about them – matching his racing colours – and whenever possible he wears an apricot rose in his buttonhole. On the day his colt Diesis won the Middle Park Stakes, his agitation as he waited on the stand was such that by the time he reached the winner's enclosure he seemed more exhausted than the horse. If he is lucky enough to own a good horse nothing would induce him to part with it; he turned down some very silly offers for Keen, the first being £2 million to be paid anywhere in the world, after he had won his first race as a two-year-old. His only grumble about the recent Arab investment in racing is that, although he welcomes the influx of some of the best young horses from the United States, he finds it disappointingly predictable that any horse who shows promise is likely to be snapped up by their agents.

Three times senior steward of the Jockey Club, Lord Howard de Walden is British racing's elder statesman. This, in addition to his business interests – he still owns some of the West End – means that he leads a hectic life. His London estate is run from offices near Harley Street, which have a superb 1930s interior: polished stone floors, polished wood on the walls, and shining tubular banisters. His own office there is more conventional; one wall is lined with a painted screen depicting a medieval battle, and the fine desk and tables are adorned with pictures of Kris and other things he cares for. He has the rare ability of not appearing to take himself, his responsibilities, or his money seriously, yet he pays more than due attention to those who deal with him. Outside racing, Lord Howard de Walden enjoys shooting and travelling – although he feels that visits to various racecourses, studs, and bloodstock sales in Australia, South Africa, and the United States mean that he does more than enough of the latter, not leaving much time for the former. He is excited by his latest purchase, a small aeroplane, which enables him to return home most evenings.

The future of horse-racing as a popular entertainment and the well-being of the thoroughbred population are both threatened by commercialization. The crucial moment came when the majority of breeders and owners were forced to treat the racehorse as a commodity. All but the very rich are now obliged by financial prudence to plan their horses' careers with a view to maximizing their value, rather than their own pleasure. That this is now the overriding intention of those lucky or skilful enough to own the best horses detracts from the spectacle of horse-racing.

For racing to be entertaining it is essential that there are equine stars, horses who dominate their contemporaries not just in one race but in a succession of races spread over two or three years. Golden Fleece may have been a great champion, but as he appeared on the racecourse only four times, he can hardly be said to have provided an enormous amount of excitement and entertainment. He was not seen on the racecourse at all after he had proved himself with brilliant success in the Derby.

British racing attracts foreign investors and popular interest, because of its variety and the atmosphere of its racecourses. The programme of any day's racing will include races over two miles or more. English racecourses are extraordinary shapes, with awkward hills and peculiar turns. Some are raced round in a clockwise direction, others anti-clockwise, while the Newmarket courses are almost completely straight. Yet the bloodstock industry now encourages specialization in a particular type of animal, specifically the horse who reaches his physical peak as a two-year-old and the horse who is at his best when racing over a mile. The succession of top two-year-olds who have failed to train on, or even to appear on the racecourse at all as three-year-olds, has taken much of the interest out of two-year-old racing. In the past it was likely that the winner of the Derby would be among the runners for the top two-year-old races, but not since The Minstrel in 1977 has a leading two-year-old winner gone on to win the Derby.

Similarly there was a time when the winners of the season's first classics – the One Thousand and Two Thousand Guineas, run at Newmarket in May over a mile – were expected to become leading contenders for the Oaks, the Derby, and other big races later in the season. The last colt to win both the Two Thousand Guineas and the Derby was Nijinsky in 1970, and Oh So Sharp in 1985 was the first filly to win the One Thousand Guineas and the Oaks since Mysterious in 1973. The follower of racing's interest in horses has always been ephemeral, with argument as to their relative merits lasting only a year or two, before the advent of a new generation. When, however, this period is reduced to a month or two, there is a danger of the whole thing becoming banal.

Specialization has also led to a paucity of both genuine stayers and sprinters. A horse has only to win the Ascot Gold Cup for it to become almost impossible to syndicate him, or to persuade breeders to send him good mares. It has been seriously suggested that the distance of all cup races should be reduced to two miles. Most top staying races are now competed for by tiny fields of moderate horses, while the best potential stayers try to prove to commercial breeders that they are middle-distance horses. If racing were to be rationalized, with the leading courses putting on meetings at which similar horses competed over similar distances, it would be very dull indeed for those not involved in the industry.

There is also a danger of future generations of thoroughbreds being adversely affected by this obsession with precocious and middle-distance horses. This is for two reasons. First, as Franco Varola has argued, it is important to preserve the different strains of the racehorse. In the long run there will always be a need for outcrops to the most fashionable blood, and the slow developing horse, the stayer, and the sprinter all have a role to play if the racehorse is to remain robust and its temperament is to remain sound. In the short run many potentially fine stallions are deprived of a chance to prove themselves, while breeders refuse to patronize staying stallions because of the difficulty of selling their offspring. A second and more imminent danger is posed by the numerous fashionable and commercially successful stallions who did not themselves possess the qualities of conformation and temperament valued in a thoroughbred racehorse.

The best example of this is the fact that almost any son of Northern Dancer, however wayward or slow, will be given a chance at stud somewhere in the world. Of his more famous sons, Shareef Dancer now stands at the Dalham Hall Stud, with a nomination fee of $150,000. Shareef Dancer ran five times in the space of ten months, winning three races and finishing second once and fourth once. On two occasions his behaviour suggested there was something wrong with his temperament; he did not appear to try when beaten in a handicap at Sandown, and before his first appearance he was led around the parade ring by a lad wearing a crash helmet while another, similarly attired, sat on his back. Besides the fact he had only one first-class performance to his name, nobody knows whether these signs of waywardness were just juvenilia or the evidence of a more serious defect.

Another example of a stallion with a dubiously high reputation is the 1984 Derby winner Secreto. Just because in one of his three races Secreto happened to stay a mile and a half better than a brilliant miler and a collection of moderate or sick horses, he is now at stud in Kentucky with a large nomination fee. It is impossible to say whether it is in the interests of the thoroughbred for horses like these to be sent some of the best broodmares available.

Commercial breeding, particularly breeding with the intention of selling the offspring as foals or yearlings, encourages a certain naïveté. The objective of realizing a high price in the sale ring overrides any long-term considerations; even the horse's ability on the racecourse takes second place. The pervasive influence of such ideals has never been better demonstrated than in an interview with Robert Sangster published in *Pacemaker International*. The interviewer asked Sangster to give an idea of the horses that Michael Dickinson will train for him in 1986, and Sangster replied that Dickinson will train some of the best of his home-bred horses. He then gave a list of some of the best racemares he has owned, together with the name of the top stallion by whom they have been covered. They may well turn out to be the best two-year-olds of 1986, but surely 200 years of carefully recorded breeding have proved that there is more to producing a good racehorse than sending the winner of the Oaks to be covered by the winner of the Derby; or, to avoid an anachronism, the winner of the Cheveley Park Stakes to the winner of the Dewhurst Stakes. Few breeders' matings today display the thought and long-term perspective that marked the operations of the Aga Khan, Lord Derby, and Marcel Boussac. And few of those who apply such qualities are in a financial position to use the best blood.

To turn to the effect of the recent changes on people who work in the racing world, those who have suffered are the small trainers, particularly in the north of England. More people own racehorses today than ever before, but the turnover of owners is also greater. The owner who patronizes a small stable can probably afford to keep only one horse, and if that fails to pay for its keep in prize money he will have to pull out.

This situation is not conducive to security for the small trainer. In order to compete for owners, many trainers charge low fees, which do not cover their costs, and hope to make up the difference through betting. Some trainers are the largest owners on their yard, attempting to cover costs by selling shares in their horses to those who cannot afford to maintain a horse on their own. Not many trainers give up, not because they exaggerate their plight, but because men like Pat Rohan and Maurice Camacho cannot contemplate any other life. They know that if they strike the 100-to-1 chance and get a good horse, they might attract new owners and break out.

Some of the discontent of stable staff with their pay is because the training of racehorses is not necessarily a profitable occupation. Stable lads are dissimilar to most other industrial wage earners: if they are good, looking after horses is much more than just a job to them. A stable lad has to work long and often irregular hours, and much of his work is done in unpleasant conditions – Newmarket is often horrible in January. Yet no stable lad will earn much. Racehorses are exercised early in the morning in order to allow the trainer, and any member of the staff who is supervising a runner, time to get to the racecourse by the afternoon. Most stables start at around seven o'clock, finishing for the morning at twelve. The lads then return to the yard at four for evening stables, which will end at about seven o'clock. The trainer, the head lad, and any lad who looks after a horse who is running that day, or whose charge is sick, will work considerably longer hours.

Most lads come into racing with the hope of becoming a jockey. Many then stay on, either because they like the life, or because by the time they realize they are not going to be a jockey they are twenty-five and not qualified to do anything else.

Of the total amount of added prize money, the top ten trainers usually win about a third. Although there is some variation in who the top ten are, there are five trainers who are always among them and perhaps another ten who often are. The lads who work in these yards are likely to be those who not only enjoy the life but are also skilled at it, and they are comparatively well paid. A percentage of the prize money a stable wins is divided among the staff, and those whose charges win races will probably receive presents from the owner. A lad who looks after a classic winner can expect a four-figure present. Many lads in these yards also make money by selling information to gamblers and bookmakers.

The economics of small training stables are different. To stay solvent it is necessary to charge low fees in order to attract owners, which leads to staff being badly paid. Many such stables now rely on girls, who do the job because they love horses.

Part of the reason why so many trainers in the north of England are in this position is their relative geographic isolation. Most of those who can afford good racehorses live in the south of England, and the bloodstock agents, who allocate the horses owned by rich foreigners, tend to be biased in favour of the south, where their homes and offices are. Another factor must be the self-image trainers project. The disdain with which 'refined' southern trainers are regarded is encapsulated in a story about the Queen's trainer, Ian Balding, that is told with pleasure in Yorkshire. Ian Balding was once taken by a Yorkshire trainer to look at some of his horses with a view to purchasing one of them. In the Land-Rover they passed some of the latter's string:

'Who are those horses?' Balding inquired politely.

'I don't know.'

'Well, are they three-year-olds, four-year-olds. . . ?'

'Never mind those buggers, let's go and look at the yearlings.'

The yearlings were in a large paddock fenced entirely with barbed wire. Unperturbed, the trainer proceeded to chase them round the paddock in the Land-Rover to see which jumped off the fastest.

The main reason for the decline in the standing of northern trainers, and for the plight of small trainers everywhere, is that to succeed as a flat trainer it is no longer sufficient to be a capable horseman. The training of racehorses is now a competitive profession, entry into which is no longer restricted by social barriers. Among today's leading trainers are Barry Hills and Clive Brittain, who both started as stable lads, a progression that was rare until recently. The leading trainers today are intelligent and well educated and often have no family background in racing. They are, in effect, businessmen, skilled at dealing with their clients and at attracting new ones. Their business is buying and marketing horses; some of the more successful expect to be given a share in any stallion they have trained. The aloofness and mutual suspicion that used to characterize trainer's dealings with each other have disappeared. For the top trainers, betting is completely irrelevant, and since they train for much the same people, the need for secrecy has diminished.

The shortest of visits to one of the top racing stables is enough to demonstrate that men like Michael Stoute, John Dunlop, Guy Harwood, and Henry Cecil are almost in a different profession to the men who train twenty or so horses. It is the scope of their operations as well as the scale. You talk to them about which of a number of possibilities will be their Derby horse, whether so-and-so will have to go to Italy to win her pattern race, or whether the prices at Keeneland will be affected by the importation ban on American bloodstock.

To run a stable with over 100 horses it is necessary to be a first-class manager, to be able to delegate, and to set up a machine that is efficient enough to run on its own while the trainer is in the United States buying yearlings, or supervising a runner in Paris. All the aspects of a trainer's job are magnified; doing the entries for his horses, finding them jockeys, and organizing transport when they run, keeping them fit and healthy and their owners happy and informed. A trainer with a large stable relies heavily upon his staff.

Guy Harwood is in many ways typical of the modern trainer. When he started training in 1966 he had no obvious qualifications for the job. His father was a successful businessman, setting up a chain of garages and an engineering firm called Spiro Gills. Harwood achieved the distinction of being the first boy from his prep school to pass the Common Entrance examination when he gained a place at Stowe. After Stowe, he spent eight years working as an engineer, before he decided to sell Spiro Gills in order to buy a farm nearby on which to start training.

Pulborough was a small Sussex village to the north of the South Downs. Like the rest of West Sussex it has now been overrun by smart detached residences, and the village has sprawled over the surrounding countryside and become a town. Guy Harwood's Coombelands Racing Stables are a surprisingly rural oasis, reached by driving out of the town on overgrown and pot-holed lanes, which receive more wear from Harwood's 150 horses than from any other traffic. To visit the stables, you turn off the lane when beckoned by a garish statue of a jockey and park in the extensive car park. The stables are centred on the office, which looks like one of the houses in the estates which lurk just over the hill. Around the office are the large American-looking barns where the horses are stabled.

Proud of the fact that he has worked up from the bottom of the profession, Harwood laughs when he recalls that in the early days it did not matter whether they won at Devon and Exeter or Folkestone, as long as they won. The whole village was excited when he had the favourite for the Lincoln Handicap in his stable, or when it was reported that the largest single bet of the year had been placed on one of his charges, Berkeley Square, when he won at Salisbury. In those days his gallops consisted of a few furlongs squeezed in between cornfields. Now he has miles of automatically watered gallops, three all-weather gallops, laid with small pieces of rubber, or sawdust, for use when the ground is frozen, and even a Tattenham Corner replica. He is always extending and improving his gallops.

Harwood has always been prepared to innovate. He has learned from experience and experimentation that a three-year-old at the top of his form weighs the same as he did in the autumn of his two-year-old days – 'Imagine telling Sir Cecil Boyd Rochfort that!' He has also been particularly successful at buying cheap horses at the sales. Young Generation, Rankin, Ela Mana Mou, and To Agori Mou were all acquired for very small amounts by today's standards. It was a great help having his own money, for this enabled him to buy yearlings whom he liked and then set about finding owners for them. He has little sympathy for the small struggling trainer – 'They ought to go out and attract owners and buy horses, not sit around complaining.' James Delahooke attributes his success to hard work: whereas most people would look at sixty horses before buying one, Harwood would look at one hundred.

'I am a trainer, not a tipster,' Harwood says; he is no longer remotely interested in betting. He considers his job as a trainer is 'to produce winners and to get the greatest potential out of the yearlings I am given'. He is ready to attribute much of his success to his staff, particularly to Geoff Lawson, his brother-in-law and assistant. In the beginning Lawson rode the odd jumper; he is now in charge of exercising the horses, leaving Harwood to deal with the entries and the owners. Harwood is also quick to praise his stable jockey, Greville Starkey, and to say how helpful their close working relationship is. He is no longer a young man – the short, swept-back hair is greying – but he cuts quite a figure in his Prince of Wales checked suits as he rushes to saddle a horse or talk to a prospective owner. It is impossible not to respect the drive, determination, and hard work that have enabled him to reach the top of his profession.

By way of contrast, Jeremy Tree is very much the old-fashioned 'gentleman trainer', a man almost in the George Lambton mould. He first became fascinated by racing when his uncle Peter Beatty's horse, Bois Roussel, won the Derby in 1938. He remembers going with him to see the horse at Beckhampton, where he was trained by Fred Darling. His aunt married an Astor, so he used to be taken to visit Lord Astor's Cliveden Stud, on outings from Eton. He was determined to be a trainer, but after leaving the army he was persuaded by his father to join a merchant bank. He did not last long in the City, taking a post as assistant trainer to Colonel Warden. A few years later he inherited his uncle's stud and set up as a trainer in Newmarket. A year later Noel Murless left Beckhampton and he was given the opportunity to take over.

Beckhampton Stables were built by Fred Darling's father. They are Victorian, of red brick, tightly enclosing a sandy courtyard and walkways. The entrance hall of the house is panelled in heavy dark wood and lined with endless black-and-white photographs of Tree's winners. The drawing room is surprisingly light in contrast, full of books, by no means all racing ones. A Munnings of his mother and brother and another of his father are on the walls, as well as a picture of Lester Piggott wearing the colours of J. H. Whitney. As he talks, Tree alternates, almost without a pause, between cigars and cigarettes, which he smokes through a holder having extracted them from a silver cigarette case.

One of the main attractions of racing for him was the glamour and social side, which he thinks no longer exists, although he admits that this is the obvious reaction of an older man. In the past he could buy cheap horses for his friends, with the possibility of them being really good, and most of the best horses were bred by their owners on their own stud farms. Today most of the best horses are owned by foreigners. In the past he could go racing safe in the knowledge that he would meet friends there; whereas today when he goes to one of the Midland meetings he will often 'not know a cat'. Characteristically, whenever he refers to an unspecified horse, he calls it 'Kiss Me Quick', and any jockey is 'K. Snooks'. Thus when explaining that he is unable to give his apprentices as many rides as he would like he says: 'It is hard to persuade an owner that K. Snooks should ride Kiss Me Quick, who cost half a million dollars.'

Tree also claims that it is no longer possible to bet, as bookmakers are scared of taking large bets from someone like himself who may be in a position to know something. He now only has five or six bets a year, although he sometimes wastes twenty-five pounds on other people's horses on the days when he does not 'know a cat', in order to relieve the boredom.

He gives the impression that there is much about racing that bores him. He loves training at Beckhampton because it is in Wiltshire, isolated from any other trainers; he would not want to be with the crowds in Newmarket, having to put up with the rumouring and gossiping and being 'drowned in racing talk'. For, as he says, he has no wish to waste his winters discussing horses. Most of his friends have nothing to do with racing, and he seldom reads the racing press. He is quite pleased to be occasionally recognized by London taxi drivers, although he puts this down to increased coverage of racing on television.

What fascinates Tree about racing today is training. He trains around fifty horses, which is more than he would really like. As he trains only for people whom he likes, he finds it difficult to say no. He has great respect for his chief patron, Khaled Abdulla, whom he describes as charming and intelligent. He has little say in the buying of Khaled Abdulla's horses, perhaps disapproving of some of the prices paid, but he is allowed to pick those he would like to train once they are assembled in England. His main aim in training is to keep his owners happy. The two things guaranteed to annoy an owner, and thus what he tries to avoid doing, are to win with their horse after telling them it has no chance, and to tell them their horse is slow even if it is really very slow.

What he enjoys about training is the atmosphere and life of a stable, the riding out in the morning, the routine, and the great excitement of having a really good horse in his care; choosing a horse as a yearling and then watching it grow, improve and fulfil its potential. He admits he finds it hard to look forward to a season unless he has one potentially top class animal in the stable, but he quickly adds that there are always the two-year-olds. Anyway with the pick of the horses that Khaled Abdulla buys or breeds, he is unlikely to have many seasons without a top class three-year-old.

Life at Beckhampton has changed little since Fred Darling's days. Tree's lads get more time off on Sundays, but they do much the same work. He disagrees with those who say that today's stable lads are inferior to those of the past; he thinks today they are better behaved than they were twenty years ago. He receives a lot of letters from boys who want to become apprentice jockeys and favours those who write from an address in the country rather than a big town. Most of his lads came to him hoping to be jockeys, but stayed on because they liked the life after any such dreams had disappeared. Ten of his lads have been with him for more than twenty-five years, and one of them worked for Fred Darling before him.

Jeremy Tree is a portly figure. He strolls around racecourses with his hands behind his back, his polished tan binocular case by his side, wearing either an ancient trilby or the sort of panama that comes from the West Indies rather than St James's. He is relaxed and likeable; his friends consider him to be a great wit. His success as a trainer is the result of one of his most apparent characteristics, which is, as Ian Balding says: 'Jeremy just loves horses.'

The others who have benefited most from racing becoming a large international business are the top jockeys, the bloodstock agents, and the many commercial middlemen in the racing world. The influence of jockeyship on the outcome of a race may only be marginal, but now that this margin can involve differences of hundreds of thousands of pounds in the valuation of a horse the rewards given to the leading jockeys have increased correspondingly. Today's top jockeys employ agents to help them secure the best rides and can expect to be given shares in the best colts they ride once they retire to stud. Lester Piggott is still pre-eminent among jockeys. If he is in a position to ignore his own and other people's contracts, it is because he is universally considered to be a great jockey.

Many jockeys have been given cause to wonder just how far Piggott will go in order to win big races. If you are ever in the happy position of owning the favourite for a classic race and the ringing of the telephone wakes you from your dreams, the chances are that it is either one of Sheikh Mohammed's agents offering you a blank cheque, or it is Piggott suggesting that rather than leaving anything to chance you should employ him for the afternoon.

The most infamous occasion of an owner agreeing to this was when it was announced two days before the 1972 Derby that Piggott and not Bill Williamson would be riding the favourite Roberto. Williamson had ridden the horse into second place in that year's Two Thousand Guineas, and although he had been injured in May he had made a good recovery and was fit to ride at Epsom. He is said to have been surprised at the news. In the race itself Rheingold looked sure to win when he went to the front a furlong from the finish, but he was hanging slightly and his jockey was unable to ride flat out. Meanwhile Roberto squeezed through a gap and under the full Piggott treatment – his whip and legs working frantically – managed to get his nose in front on the line.

Piggott had ridden a great race, but he was led into the winner's enclosure in a silence broken only by a few embarrassed cheers from those who had backed him. Williamson was given a great ovation when he won the next race. Mrs Piggott remarked, after her husband had won the 1983 Derby on Teenoso, that it was nice for Lester to win the Derby on a horse whom no one else was expecting to ride.

Perhaps the most surprising thing about Piggott, considering how easy it would be for him to be arrogant or for others to envy him, is how well liked he is. He is said to be very popular with his fellow jockeys, and most of those owners and trainers who might have most cause to be annoyed speak of him with a genuine affection, even if some of them are content to find someone else to ride their horses. It is generally thought that if he can ever bring himself to give up riding he will be a successful trainer, as he is an intelligent man and possesses the ability to understand horses. His friends consider him to be excellent company and he is known for his sharp wit.

Of the many apocryphal Piggott stories, one is that after the 1984 Derby, in which many considered Pat Eddery had ridden an injudicious race on the favourite El Gran Señor, he went up to the horse's trainer, Vincent O'Brien, and remarked: 'Missed me then, did you, Vincent?' He is also said to have rung up Darrel McHargue in the week of the 1984 St Leger, after he had persuaded the owner of the favourite, Commanche Run, that he and not McHargue should ride the horse. McHargue arrived at the telephone out of breath to say he was sorry but he could not talk as he was in the middle of a game of tennis. Piggott is reputed to have replied that it was all right, as he was only ringing to tell him that he would be playing tennis on Saturday. Piggott and Commanche Run won the St Leger that Saturday.

Lester Piggott may have achieved a level of independence and financial success that will never be emulated, but the services of men like Steve Cauthen and Pat Eddery are demanded by most owners and trainers in the country. Such men attract crowds to the meetings at which they ride.

The commercial middlemen in the racing world have benefited both from the increased value of bloodstock and from the new international stance of the industry. The large bloodstock agencies now offer a wide range of services; they buy and sell horses, organize transport abroad and insurance, carry out pedigree research, and help manage and promote stallions. The British Bloodstock Agency is now a public company, with its shares quoted on the Stock Exchange. There are also many companies that specialize in each of these fields, and the sales companies have been making record profits in recent years.

The general air of prosperity at the top of the bloodstock industry is such that it is not obvious why it should matter that some have suffered from the changes of the last ten years. Horse-racing and breeding are now a competitive, international business, and if the small and unsuccessful men at the bottom are being squeezed out, some may consider that this can only be in the long-term interests of the industry. It may be unfortunate and some may suffer but, the argument runs, this is the inevitable consequence of recent international developments. Such a rationale has a degree of support among those at the top of the industry, but it is founded upon false reasoning and a false sense of security.

Horse-racing and breeding in Britain rely completely upon foreigners and foreign investment. This has never been more obvious than in 1984, when of the twelve leading owners in terms of prize money won only three lived in England, one of whom was Captain Marcos Lemos, a Greek. Yet with the exception of Luigi Miglitti, the owner of Secreto, they all maintain a number of horses in training in Britain. The reasons why foreigners choose to support British racing are, as we have seen, probably the result of its historical standing and traditional veneer, the atmosphere of British racecourses, and the diversity of their programmes. If these are the major factors in the appeal British racing has for foreigners, then it is in the interests of everyone in the racing world, and those who look to racing for entertainment, to ensure they are maintained.

However, as we have also observed, there are many ways in which the bloodstock industry creates financial pressures that work against this aim. The atmosphere on British racecourses, and the general appeal of the racing world, will be seriously damaged if the small breeder, the small owner, and the small trainer are forced to withdraw from the industry. The popularity and interest stimulated by horses like Soba and Mighty Flutter reinforce this point: both were unfashionably bred, raced by their breeders, and trained in small yards, yet both came close to winning Group One races. Similarly the appeal of horse-racing is diminished by the growing specialization of the thoroughbred: neither horses who retain their form for a few months, nor endless races run over similar distances, generate much excitement or public interest.

The disappearance of the traditional veneer of horse-racing is less of a cause for concern. Over the years, the benign effect of attracting foreign investment has probably been outweighed by the damaging effects of managerial and administrative incompetence. Racing long since ceased to be a sport, or an indulgence of the rich, and attempts to preserve this impression have been increasingly hypocritical and self-defeating.

Horse-racing in the United States relies more upon a large number of owner-dealers than upon foreign investment. This is partly because the United States is a more prosperous nation than Britain, but it is also the result of the tax incentives offered to American racehorse owners. In the United States it is possible to set losses incurred through owning racehorses against profits made in another business, for tax purposes. To qualify for this an owner has only to make a profit from his racing twice every seven years; thus many American owners sell much of their stock twice every seven years. Such incentives are unlikely to be introduced in Britain, so for the foreseeable future British racing will rely upon foreigners and those who can afford to race only on a small scale.

The man who spends $150,000 on having his mare covered by a stallion may not see much connection between his business and what happens at Folkestone on a Monday in April. Nevertheless, the whole bloodstock industry depends upon racing remaining appealing to watch and to gamble on. There is a danger that those in the racing world expect their audience to be as obsessed with racing as they are. To many who follow racing, a collection of elderly handicappers running over two miles is more interesting than watching expensive and highly bred two-year-olds, most of whom will be at stud within the year. Every Secreto and Shareef Dancer diminishes the appeal of racing as a spectacle. The bloodstock industry should realize that the divergence of their aims from those of the entertainment industry will eventually damage both. There is a general false sense of security in the bloodstock world, and today's apparent prosperity rests upon unstable foundations. Besides the detrimental effect commercial breeding has on the future development of the thoroughbred, and the fact that many commercial breeders do not make money, the whole industry relies upon there being rich men prepared to waste money on horses. The bloodstock world is beginning to resemble the art world, with a lot of dealers selling their stock to one another and the only man who makes money being the one who finally sells to an outsider. The advertising and promotion of stallions undoubtedly have beneficial effects, but who is fooled by a bogus reputation? Surely those in the trade are aware of the respective merits and potentiality of stallions?

There is already a worldwide problem of overproduction in the bloodstock industry, and some of its participants may have expanded rashly. If there was a revolution in Dubai, or Robert Sangster were to go bust, both unlikely but possible events, then much of the spectacular commercial activity of the last few years would appear foolish.

The last ten years have been the first phase of horse-racing as an international business. When Sangster and the Arabs begin to breed on a large scale, it is to be expected that their acquisition of horses will be less rapacious. The bloodstock market will not collapse, for any large breeding operation will need to go to the market continually, to sell and buy new stock. There must be a chance that the market will at least stabilize and the value of bloodstock will not continue to rise annually. Possibly, too, long-term objectives will again be introduced into breeding, with Khaled Abdulla's operation being the most likely stabilizing influence.

Frequently during its history, racing in Britain has appeared to rely dangerously upon one or two men, and yet there has been a succession of rich men prepared to indulge in ownership. It is unlikely that any prophecy of a general collapse will be fulfilled. Nevertheless it is important for the racing world to move with the times, to be aware that it is an entertainment industry, and one that relies upon foreign investment.

Notes

1 The Golden Age of English Racing

1   The English Triple Crown is made up of the Two Thousand Guineas, the Derby, and the St Leger. All three races are confined to three-year-olds, and a horse that wins all three is said to have won the Triple Crown. The remaining classic races – the One Thousand Guineas and the Oaks – are confined to three-year-old fillies.
2   Cited in Abram S. Hewitt, *The Great Breeders and their Methods*, Thoroughbred Publishers Inc., 1982
3   Richard Marsh, *A Trainer to Two Kings*, Cassell, 1925
4   Charles Morton, *My Sixty Years of the Turf*, Hutchinson, 1930

2 Tradition and Change

1   George Lambton, *Men and Horses I have known*, J.A. Allen, 1963
2   Cited in Michael Seth Smith, *The Classic Connection*, Secker & Warburg, 1983
3   Richard Marsh, op. cit.
4   Michael Seth Smith, op. cit.
5   George Lambton, op. cit.
6   Ibid.
7   Franco Varola, *Typology of the Racehorse*, J.A. Allen, 1977

3 The New Rich

1   Sir Gordon Richards, *My Story*, Hodder & Stoughton, 1955
2   The Jameson raid of 1895–6 was a bungled attempt at a *coup d'état* in South Africa inspired by Cecil Rhodes. It had the support of the English business community there.
3   Sir Harry Preston, *Leaves from my Unwritten Diary*, Hutchinson, 1936

4 Steve Ahern, *Riches from Horses*, Stanley Paul, 1964
5 Sidney Galtrey, *Memoirs of a Racing Journalist*, Hutchinson, 1934
6 Sir Alfred Munnings, *Autobiography* (3 vols), Museum Press, 1950–52

4 Jockeys and Trainers

1 Sir Alfred Munnings, op. cit.
2 Charlie Smirke, *Finishing Post*, Oldbourne, 1960
3 Tommy Weston, *My Racing Life*, Hutchinson, 1952
4 Eph Smith, *Riding to Win*, Stanley Paul, 1968
5 Marcus Marsh, *Racing with the Gods*, Pelham Books, 1968
6 Doug Smith, *Five Times Champion*, Pelham Books, 1968
7 The Lonsdale Sporting Library, *Flat Racing*, Earl of Harewood and Lt-Col P.E. Ricketts (eds), Seeley Service & Co, 1940

5 The Aga Khan

1 Vuillier started his research by taking the pedigrees of 100 major winners back twelve generations. His method was then to assume the total dosage of each generation was one. To find out the dosage of St Simon in a particular horse, you would count 1/4 if St Simon appeared once among the grandparents, and 1/4,096 if he appeared once in the twelth generation; or 3/64 if he appeared three times in the sixth generation, in which there are sixty-four ancestors. He found that, after a time, the dosage of certain stallions appearing in the pedigree of leading winners tended towards a constant, but this constant differed from stallion to stallion. The dosage constant for St Simon was about twice as high as that of Bend Or. Vuillier's idea was that in breeding the objective should be for the foal to have the closest possible figure for the great stallions, to the constant for leading winners. Thus if a stallion's figures were too high in St Simon, he should be mated with a mare having a deficiency of St Simon figures. It is generally thought today that any ancestor further removed than the third generation is an irrelevance.
2 Leonard Slater, *Aly: A Biography*, W.H. Allen, 1966
3 Ibid.
4 H.J. Greenwall, *His Highness The Aga Khan*, Cresset Press, 1952

6 The French Era

1 The Prix du Jockey Club is the French equivalent of the Derby, run at Chantilly over a mile and a half. The Prix de Diane is the French equivalent of the Oaks, run over a mile and a quarter also at Chantilly, in June.

7   The Challenge of Change

1   R. Black, *The Jockey Club and its Founders*, Smith Elder & Co, 1891
2   R. Mortimer, R. Onslow, P. Willett, *Biographical Encyclopaedia of British Flat Racing*, Macdonald & Jane's, 1978

Bibliography

Acton, C.R., *Silk and Spur*, Richards, 1935

Aga Khan III, Sultan Mohammed Shah Aga Khan, *The Memoirs of the Aga Khan*, Cassell, 1954

Ahern, Steve, *Riches from Horses*, Stanley Paul, 1964

Bebbington, W., *Rogues go Racing*, Good & Betts, 1947

Blakeborough, John Freeman Fairfax, *Paddock Personalities*, Hutchinson, 1935

    Sykes of Sledmere, P. Allan, 1929

    Turf's Who's Who, Periodical Publications, 1932

Bland, Ernest, *Flat Racing since 1900*, Andrew Dakers, 1950

Booth, J.B., *Bits of Character. A Life of Henry Hall Dixon*, Hutchinson, 1936

    Life, Laughter and Brass Hats, T. Werner Laurie, 1939

Britt, Edgar, *Post Haste; As told to Gerald Pynt*, Muller, 1967

Browne, T.H., *History of the English Turf, 1904–1930*, Virtue & Co, 1931

Bull, Phil, *The Mathematics of Betting*, Morrison & Gibb, 1945

Carr, Harry, *Queen's Jockey*, Stanley Paul, 1966

Childs, Joe, *My Racing Reminiscences*, Hutchinson's Library of Sports & Pastimes, 1952

Churchill, Randolph S., *Lord Derby*, Heinemann, 1959

Cook, Sir Theodore, *Character and Sportsmanship*, Williams & Norgate, 1927

Craig, Dennis, *Horse-Racing*, J.A. Allen, 1963

Curling, B.W.R., *The Captain: a Biography of Captain Sir Cecil Boyd Rochfort*, Barrie & Jenkins, 1970

    Derby Double: the Unique Story of Racehorse Trainer Arthur Budgett, Luscombe, 1977

Darling, Sam, *Reminiscences*, Mills & Boon, 1914

Dawson, Elizabeth, *Mother made a Book*, Geoffrey Bles, 1962

Dawson, Captain L., *Lonsdale, The Authorized Life of Hugh Lowther, Fifth Earl of Lonsdale*, Odhams Press, 1946

Devonshire, Andrew, Duke of, *Park Top: A Romance of the Turf*, London Magazine Editions, 1976

Dighton, Adair, *My Sporting Life*, Richards, 1934

Donoghue, Steve, *Donoghue Up!*, Collins, 1938
    Just My Story, Hutchinson, 1923

FitzGerald, Arthur, *History of the Prix de l'Arc de Triomphe, 1965–82*, Sidgwick & Jackson, 1983

Galtrey, Sidney, *Memoirs of a Racing Journalist*, Hutchinson, 1934

Gilbey, Quintin, *Champions all: Steve to Lester*, Hutchinson, 1971
    Fun Was My Living, Hutchinson, 1970
    Winners and Losers, Welbecson Press, 1929

Good, Meyrick, *The Lure of the Turf*, Odhams Press, 1957

Greenwall, H.J., *His Highness The Aga Khan, Imam of the Ismailis*, Cresset Press, 1952

Gribble, Philip, *Off the Cuff*, Phoenix House, 1964

Hewitt, Abram S. *The Great Breeders and their Methods*, Thoroughbred Publishers Inc., 1982

Hicks, Sir Edward Seymour, *Vintage Years*, Cassell, 1943

Hislop, John, *The Brigadier: The Story of Brigadier Gerard*, Secker & Warburg, 1973
    Far from a Gentleman, Michael Joseph, 1960
    Racing Reflections, Hutchinson, 1955

Humphris, E.M., *The Life of Mathew Dawson*, H.F. & G. Witherby, 1928

Jackson, Stanley, *The Aga Khan, Prince, Prophet, and Statesman*, Odhams Press, 1952
    The Sassoons, Heinemann, 1968

Jacobson, Arthur, *Huic Holloa!*, Sampson Low, 1935

Joel, Stanhope, *Ace of Diamonds*, Frederick Muller, 1958

Johnstone, Rae, *The Rae Johnstone Story*, Stanley Paul, 1958

Kaye, Richard, *The Ladbrokes Story*, Pelham Books, 1969

Khan, Dr Paul, *The Sport of Kings: a Study of Traditional Social Structures under Change*, (unpublished), Ph.D Swansea, 1980

Lambton, George, *Men and Horses I have known*, J.A. Allen, 1963

Lawrence, John, *The Story of Mill Reef*, Michael Joseph, 1974

The World of Racing, Purnell, 1970

Leach, Jack, *Sods I have cut on the Turf*, Victor Gollancz, 1961

    A Rider on the Stand, Stanley Paul, 1970

Llewellyn, Sir Rhys, *Breeding to Race*, J.A. Allen, 1965

Longrigg, Roger, *The History of Horse Racing*, Macmillan, 1972

Lyle, R.C., *The Aga Khan's Horses*, Putnam, 1938

    Brown Jack, Putnam, 1934

    Royal Newmarket, Putnam, 1945

Marsh, Marcus, *Racing with the Gods*, Pelham Books, 1968

Marsh, Richard, *A Trainer to Two Kings*, Cassell, 1925

Milnes, R.O.A., Marquis of Crewe, *Lord Rosebery*, John Murray, 1931

Moorhouse, Edward, *The Romance of the Derby*, Biographical Press, 1908

Mortimer, Roger, *The Flat*, Allen & Unwin, 1979

    The History of the Derby Stakes, Michael Joseph, 1973

    The Jockey Club, Cassell, 1958

Mortimer, Roger, Richard Onslow and Peter Willett, *Biographical Encyclopaedia of British Flat Racing*, Macdonald and Jane's, 1978

Morton, Charles, *My Sixty Years of the Turf*, Hutchinson, 1930

Munnings, Sir Alfred, *An Artist's life. (The Second Burst; The Finish)*, Museum Press, 1950–52

Nevill, Ralph, *The Sport of Kings*, Methuen, 1926

Newton, Alfred E., *Derby Day and Other Adventures*, L. Dickson & Thompson, 1935

Oakeshott, Michael, and Guy T. Griffith, *A Guide to the Classics or How to Pick the Derby Winner*, Faber & Faber, 1936

Onslow, Richard, *Headquarters; A History of Newmarket and its Racing*, Great Ouse Press, Cambridge, 1983

Orchard, V., *Tattersalls*, Hutchinson, 1953

Porter, John, with Edward Moorhouse, *John Porter of Kingsclere*, Grant Richards, 1919

Portland, The Sixth Duke of, *Memoirs of Racing and Hunting*, Faber & Faber, 1935

Preston, Sir Harry, *Leaves from my Unwritten Diary*, Hutchinson 1936

Rickman, Eric, *Come Racing with Me*, Chatto & Windus, 1951

    On and Off the Racecourse, G. Routledge & Sons, 1937

Rodrigo, Robert, *The Paddock Book*, MacDonald, 1967

The Racing Game, Phoenix Sports Books, 1958

Sarl, Arthur S., *Gamblers of the Turf*, Hutchinson, 1938

Sievier, R.S., *The Autobiography of Robert Standish Sievier*, Winning Post, 1906

Siltzer, Frank, *Newmarket: its Sport and Personalities*, Cassell, 1923

Slater, Leonard, *Aly: A Biography*, W.H. Allen, 1966

Sloan, J.F., *Tod Sloan. By Himself*, Grant Richards, 1915

Smirke, Charlie, *Finishing Post*, Oldbourne, 1960

Smith, Doug, with Peter Willett, *Five Times Champion*, Pelham Books, 1968

Smith, Eph, *Riding To Win*, Stanley Paul, 1968

Smith, Michael Seth, *Steve. The Life and Times of Steve Donoghue*, Faber & Faber, 1974

Urquhart, Alastair, *The Wit of the Turf*, Frewin, 1972

Vamplew, Wrag, *The Turf*, Allen Lane, 1976

Varola, Franco, *The Functional Development of the Thoroughbred*, J.A. Allen, 1980

    Typology of the Racehorse, J.A. Allen, 1977

Watson, Alfred E.T., *A Great Year*, Longmans Green & Co, 1921

Weston, Tommy, *My Racing Life*, Hutchinson's Library of Sports & Pastimes, 1952

White, Sidney H., *I gotta Horse. The Autobiography of Ras Prince Monolulu*, Hurst & Blackett, 1950

Willett, Peter, *An Introduction to the Thoroughbred*, Stanley Paul, 1966

    The Classic Racehorse, Stanley Paul, 1981

    The Thoroughbred, Weidenfeld & Nicolson, 1970

Wood, R.W. *Cavalcade of Racing*, Postlib Publications, 1947

X, Captain, *Tales of the Turf*, Partridge Publications, 1944

Young, George, *Golden Prince*, Robert Hale, 1955

Index